The Goodger Guide to the Pug

by

Wilhelmina Swainston-Goodger

Classic Dog Book Series

OTR Publications

THE GOODGER GUIDE TO THE PUG
ISBN 0-940-269-11-2

© 1995 by OTR Publications

All Rights Reserved. No part of this book may be reproduced or transmitted in any form or by any means, electronic or mechanical, including photocopying, recording or by any information storage or retrieval system—except by a review to be printed in a magazine or newspaper—without permission from the publisher.

Library of Congress Cataloging-in-Publication Data

Swainston-Goodger, Wilhelmina.
    The Goodger guide to the pug / by Wilhelmina Swainston-Goodger
       p.   cm. --(Classic dog book series)
    Contains: The pug dog, its history and origin; and. The pug handbook
    Includes bibliographical references (p.   ).
    ISBN 0-940269-11-2
      1. Pug. I. Swainston-Goodger, Wilhelmina. Pug dog, its history and origin. II. Swainston-Goodger, Wilhelmina. Pug handbook. III. Title. IV. Series.
SF429.P9S88   1995
636.7' 6--dc20
                                                                                            95-37184
                                                                                               CIP

Printed in the United States of America

10 9 8 7 6 5 4 3 2 1

The books reprinted in this volume were originally published in 1930 and 1959. The practical information, particularly with regard to breeding, feeding, management, housing and treatment of diseases and/or ailments may be out-of-date. They are included here ONLY for their historical value. Please consult your veterinarian before following any of the advice contained herein. We assume no responsibility for errors, inaccuracies, omissions or any inconsistency herein. Any slights of people or organizations are unintentional.

OTR PUBLICATIONS
P.O. Box 481
Centreville, AL 35042

Contents

Introduction 5
by Cathy J. Flamholtz

BOOK ONE
THE PUG DOG, ITS HISTORY AND ORIGIN

Preface 11

1. Origin Theories 17

2. China 27

3. Holland 35

4. 17th & 18th Century England 45

5. France and Italy 59

6. 19th Century England 67

7. Black and Other Coloured Pugs 91

8. The 20th Century Pug 99

9. The Pug in America 105

10. Show Points 115

11. Footnotes 120

BOOK TWO
THE PUG HANDBOOK

Preface 127

1. Origin 129
The Pug Skull • Early Importations

2. History 143
China • Europe • England • Black Dogs

3. Some Early Show Dogs 159

4. Contemporary Dogs 167

5. Formation of the Pug Dog Club 177

6. The Standard 179
Diagram • Points

7. Breeding 187
Mating • Whelping

8. Feeding 199
Weaning • Puppy Feeding • Adult Feeding

9. Management 207
Kennelling • Exercise • House Training • Grooming and Bathing • Ailments

10. Exhibiting 223
Classes • Definitions of Classes

11. Footnotes 232

12. A Selected Bibliography 235

Introduction

While researching one of my books, I chanced upon a copy of Mrs. Wilhelmina Swainston-Goodger's *The Pug Dog, Its Origin and History,* published in 1930, the first British book on the breed. I finished reading the book in one sitting. I was immediately impressed by Mrs. Goodger's love for the Pug. Indeed, it shone from every page in the book. But, that can be said for many writers. What set this work apart from other breed books was Mrs. Goodger's relentless scholarship on the Pug's history. Most other writers repeat *ad infinitum* the commonly accepted history of their breed. They quote from and accept the conclusions of early cynologists. Not so Mrs. Goodger. Whenever she came across a quote about the Pug, she donned her detective's cap and persistently tracked down the lead, attempting to discover its genesis. She did not confine her research, as so many others have done, to dog books alone. Books on history, biographies, art and pottery, anything that could shed light on the true history of the Pug...she doggedly pursued them all.

"...the intention (of this book) is to give a short history of the breed during the 2600 years or so of its known existence," Mrs. Goodger writes. How well she succeeded. As a result of her extraordinary work, she shed new light on what we know about the breed, separating the "solemn nonsense," as she termed it, from the truth. Many other writers are loathe to state their actual conclusions on subjects, to step up to the plate and take a stand on their convictions. Mrs. Goodger was confident in her research and her conclusions are logical, well-founded and always rooted firmly in fact. She set a very high standard for all future breed historians...one that has rarely been equaled.

Unfortunately, *The Pug Dog, Its Origin and History* has become a collector's item. It commands steep prices in the catalogues of those who deal in antiquarian dog books. This has deprived many modern Pug fanciers of the opportunity to appreciate the brilliance of Mrs. Goodger's work.

In 1959, Mrs. Goodger wrote *The Pug Handbook,* as one volume in a series of such books on many breeds. She added valuable new information on history...items she had discovered since the publication of her 1930 work. As one reads the book, however, it is clear that she was constrained by the dictates of her publisher: the chapters and lengths that they wanted included in the book. One can clearly feel her straining at the imposed bonds, with the desire to say more, more, more!

Despite the restrictions, however, we learn many new things in *The Pug Handbook.* In addition to the valuable historical additions, we hear Mrs. Goodger's views on raising dogs. Some of her feelings on this matter are unique and charming. It's true that some are now outdated and you should always check with your vet or modern breeders before following her advice. Some of the material, however, is still valuable and sage. Modern Pug owners will, once again, be impressed by Mrs. Goodger's love for her chosen breed.

"Pugs, like all articles of first-rate quality, do not inspire neutral feelings: people either adore or detest them," Mrs. Goodger writes. I would elaborate further. People who don't know the Pug may detest it from afar. Those who have lived with one of these dogs or been fortunate enough to spend time in their presence, are soon won over. I well remember taking my first Pug to a friend's house. Visiting was a German Shepherd man who looked down his nose at any non-working breed. While we talked, I tossed a ball across the room. Jackie, my Pug, gleefully retrieved it to hand. When I was busy talking, she did not interrupt. Instead, she threw the ball into the air herself and caught it precisely. What joy and delight she took in her game. Slowly, a smile came to the lips of my Shepherd owning friend. "Sure wish my dogs would show such enthusiasm," he said. "I must admit I've never liked Pugs, and often made fun of the people who own them. Now I understand their appeal. They just don't act like toy dogs." By the time we left, he had fallen under the spell of the breed. "Maybe

I should get a Pug. It would be nice to have a small dog. Do you think they'd get along with Shepherds?" I could only laugh. Jackie, as so many thousands of Pugs before and after her, had charmed this big burly man. "...the Pug is referred to as 'multim in parvo,' and though this strictly only describes his appearance," Mrs. Goodger writes, "I like to translate it as 'the little dog that has so much.'" All Pug owners would certainly agree.

Who was this outstanding writer? Wilhelmina Swainston-Goodger owned the Swainston Kennels. For a period of an astounding 69 years, she produced Champion and Challenge Certificate winning Pugs. Her most notable dog was Ch. Thunder-Cloud of Swainston. First shown before his first birthday, he topped the breed at Crufts and won his first Challenge Certificate. On the next day, he was selected Best Toy Dog and won the International Toy Dog Trophy. He continued to rack up the wins. He was Best in Show at the National Specialties in 1938 and 1939. He topped Crufts in both those years, also. In fact, while he was campaigning, he was never defeated. Sadly, the war interrupted his show career and we are left to only wonder at the record he would have achieved. When dog shows resumed in England, in 1946, Mrs. Goodger brought the then nine-year old dog out again. The veteran took second and reserve at the National Specialty, the only time he was bested by another dog. Pug breeders of the time proclaimed him "Pug of the Century."

Some will remember Wilhelmina Swainston-Goodger as a legendary breeder, but her enduring legacy is really to be found in her magnificent writing. For the first time, her works are joined together, here, in a single volume for all to enjoy. OTR Publications would like to thank Clifford Hubbard, of Wales, the original editor for *The Pug Handbook,* for allowing us to purchase the rights to that book and, therefore, join Mrs. Goodger's works. The books appear just as she wrote them. However, we have made some additions. As was typical of many early breed books, *The Pug Dog, Its Origin and History,* included only a single illustration. We have supplemented the text with additional photos and prints. I hope you enjoy these volumes as much as I have.

Cathy J. Flamholtz
July, 1995

"Alsatians, indeed!" snorted a fat pug-dog through his ridiculously inadequate nose. "We'll show 'em!" And he threw off the woollen shawl in which he had reclined like some one simply thirsting for a fight.

"Perhaps I may not see the day when our respectable old English race will hunt Alsatians out of the country, but *you* will," and he turned round to a litter of corkscrew-tailed pups in the next cage.

"Wather, wather," yapped the youngsters, treading on each other's backs in their excitement.

"That's the spirit," approved the veteran.

The Daily Mirror, 1927

His face is distinctly his fortune with other dogs. There is something about the pug complexion which depresses quite big dogs, and a favourite jest among pug pups is to look steadily at an Alsatian and watch him run for miles.

Northern Dispatch, 1930

The Pug Dog

Its History and Origin

by

Wilhelmina Swainston-Goodger

Dedicated

to the memory of

Swainston Gabrielle

a worthy member of the

'Grand Little Breed'

Preface

> "At morning's call,
> The small-voiced Pug-dog welcomes in the sun,
> And flea-bit mongrels, wakening one by one,
> Give answer all."
>
> O. W. HOLMES.

HE pug-dog is one of the earliest breeds of dog—in fact, so far as I can trace, it carries its history back for a longer period than any other breed except the greyhound. The greyhound is generally admitted, without question, to be the earliest extant type of dog, and J. Maxtee, in his *Popular Toy-Dogs: Their Breeding, Exhibition and Management,* published in 1922, upholds this theory when writing of pug-dogs:

> "Pugs are of far more ancient date than is popularly supposed.... There is ample existing evidence of this in the museums and elsewhere, on the sculptures, etc.; and although I am not inclined to say that they are as old as the Greyhound, I nevertheless favour the idea that for antiquity such dogs run the latter very close— so close, in fact, that it is difficult to separate the one from the other in point of age."

So far as England is concerned there are few breeds having so long an historical connection with this country, being almost continually under Royal patronage; and they certainly appear to be the second oldest breed of toy-dog, lap-spaniels of various denominations preceding them.

With all breeds of dog the question of intelligence is an important feature. Toy-dogs, having more of human association, are in general more humanly intelligent than their outdoor brothers, which makes it difficult to draw a comparison between them. It would certainly be easier to train a young retriever to retrieve game than it would be to train a pug-dog to do so, whereat a sportsman might regard the retriever as being a more intelligent breed than the pug-dog; but, in the house, as a house dog, the pug-dog admits no superiors. He is not only exceptionally quick of hearing but his bark, unlike many other toy-dogs, is a pleasing tone to the ear, being deep and full, which convinces a stranger that there is a big dog in the house; and, he does not bark unless he means it. There is no continuous and useless yapping at the gate, for instance.

On the stage he has come into competition with the poodle, by many people given the name of being the most intelligent dog, because of his almost uncanny knack of learning tricks; but the pug-dog has in many cases met and defeated the poodle on his own ground.

I certainly claim that there is no breed that can compete with the pug-dog in a question of general intelligence, especially in understanding the moods of his owner and accommodating himself to them—for either a tramp in the country or a *siesta* in front of the fire. He is ever ready when you are.

So far as popularity goes, he has twice been the most popular dog in England: once during the mid-eighteenth century, and once during the mid-Victorian era. The third time is approaching. He is, at present, the third most popular toy, so far as registrations[1] go, both in this country and in the U.S.A.

Until the coming of black pug-dogs in the late nineteenth century he was always a fawn-coloured dog with a black mask on his face, a black line, or trace, down his back, and a similar marking spreading across it at the shoulders known as a "saddle-mark." His fawn varied in shades, but the early specimens were golden or apricot fawns. Later the pepper-and-salts, or smutty fawns, were introduced. Tastes in a fancy change just as fashions do. At the present day the trace and saddlemark are not so much insisted upon. These points were always more marked in the pepper-and-salts, or Willoughbys, as they used to be called. As far as fawns are concerned, the clear fawns, or Morrisons of the old day, seem to be the most favoured at the present time. We may have lost some of the trace and saddle-mark, but modern breeders have certainly succeeded in producing shorter faces without altering the noble character of the head.

It is very remarkable that the pug-dog should have kept up its distinctive form for so long. There is no difference between the earliest specimens and those of the present day, apart from improvements brought about by better conditions and selective breeding. There is not, I believe, one other breed of dog of which the same thing can be said. Many breeds have kept to distinctive types but few, if any, to distinctive details. It is really remarkable that in any breed any distinction at all should have been kept up, as no real interest in the points of dogs or in their pedigrees was taken till the nineteenth century, when dog-shows first made their appearance. From after that date people were compelled to breed up to a definite type, and in many cases (alas, how many ?) inbreeding was the only result.

The pug-dog may claim his distinctive type in that he always keeps aloof from other breeds. He is not courageous with other dogs, which is, in my opinion, a distinct advantage, and it is probably through this that he is so seldom inflicted with that canine scourge, distemper. For many years I have enjoyed the society of pug-dogs, and for some eight years I have been breeding them; yet, I have never had a pug-dog with distemper, and, so far as I have heard, none of the puppies I have sold have suffered from that disease. A case in point is that of a four-months-old puppy of mine who went to some people in the south. They had an Airedale terrier which was suffering from distemper, though the fact was not discovered until the day before the arrival of the puppy. The Airedale was sent to the veterinary surgeon, but, apart from this, no process of disinfection or other precautions were taken. Yet, the puppy marched, as it were, straight into the Airedale's distemper-infected shoes and remained absolutely unscathed. I may add that the Airedale had been allowed the run of the house during the day, and that the pug-dog therefore lived and lay in exactly the same spots as had been lived and lain in by the sick dog. I do not, of course, claim that pug-dogs are immune from distemper; they certainly are not, but it is rare amongst them.

As house dogs they are admirable. They are naturally clean and almost wholly free from "doggy" smell. There can be no question about them being excellent watch-dogs. One thing that is not generally known is that they are exceptionally hardy, and the way the breed has thrived in Russia proves that the cold does not daunt them. This does not mean that they can be treated without any consideration at all and be expected to survive. Pug-dogs, like other breeds, must be treated with discernment in accordance with their physical and mental individualities. It is a fact that outdoor kennelling has proved successful in the South of England, but, the happiness of the dog being considered, I would not personally advise this method with pug-dogs, for the best results. Another important point of advantage that the pug-dog possesses over all long- coated breeds is emphasised by our uncertain English climate; his short coat can be dried in a minute, and his *toilette is* a matter which would never cause pricks of conscience to those busy people who, fond as they are of their pets, often have a hundred and one other things to do besides the grooming of their dogs. The pug-dog is always smart and trim, and he keeps sweet and clean without the number of baths required by some of the other breeds. Many pug-dog lovers prefer the weekly grooming (all that is necessary) and seldom, if ever, bath their pug-dogs at all.

The pug-dog, if I may say so, is almost too perfect in associationship with children. This, of course, is perhaps to the dog's disadvantage, but certainly to the child's advantage. The breed is very popular, especially with young children, their velvety softness and their obviously comical appearance makes a direct appeal to the child heart, and careful grown-ups will not need to think twice of the advantage possessed by the pug-dog in his cleanliness and freedom from smell (for which he is deservedly famous). Everybody knows the fame of the canine races in general for their love and complete understanding of children. It is as if they knew that man's child was their worshipped master's most precious possession, but, apart from this, there is a camaraderie between the child and the dog from which the man, even if he be the master, often finds himself excluded. The pug-dog's unfailing good nature and absolute devotion to the object of his affection makes him an ideal companion for the child. There have been cases where the pug-dog has suffered martyrdoms at the hands of a child sooner than retaliate, which seems very sad to me, although I am just as much child-lover as I am canine enthusiast.

In extracts in this book taken from a letter of Mr. Mayhew and from the works of Mr. Lee you will see that each of these gentlemen knew of pug-dogs with distinctly sporting turns of mind. I have a little black bitch who also thoroughly enjoys rabbiting, and who goes out shooting with my husband without being in the least gun-shy. This little dog was once lost for a week in December on the moors near Newcastle, sleeping out in the very frosty air. Apart from slight skin trouble, picked up on this outing, she suffered no ill-effects. More recently, in late October, she was caught by the foot in a rabbit snare on the Cheviot Hills, and though search was made for her all night she was not discovered till eight o'clock the next morning, being in the snare for roughly fifteen hours. Beyond a few tears and a great show of gratitude to the person who unsnared her she showed no ill-effects whatsoever. There could hardly have been a better example of the hardiness of the breed or of its patience under adverse circumstances.

Some breeders claim that the black pug-dog is hardier than the fawn. I think this is questionable, but I have given a rather amusing extract with regard to this, written under the pseudonym, "La Vedette," in the chapter on blacks. "La Vedette" is perfectly right in substance, regarding the fawn pug-dog's aversion to wet weather, though, I think, he rather exaggerates it. The fawn dog is much like the average human being in this respect. He likes his comfort. It is more the thought of the chilly outing that rankles. Once the walk has started he enjoys himself as much as any other dog. Like everything else, it is all a matter of habit. Fawn pug-dogs who are taken for a regular walk every day show little reluctance at leaving the room and fireplace, whereas those who are taken out at irregular intervals might well be sympathised with should they infer that a fine day would have been more suitable for the abandonment of their cosy corner! However, this aspersion, if it is an aspersion, could never under any circumstances be cast on the blacks. Let it rain or snow, Mr. Black Pug-Dog is just as happy, and would not miss his walk for any storm. He has all the small child's passion for paddling in muddy puddles, but he comes back after his walk in the rain, glowing and full of vigour, his lovely jetty satin coat looking more beautiful than ever, after a brisk rub-down.

Considering the historical association of the pug-dog with this country it is really rather remarkable that no book has been published on the breed in England. The Americans have their book by Dr. Cryer, but, apart from references to the pug-dog in canine text-books, no book has been written on the breed, either descriptive or historical. This present little book is a very cursory history of the breed, but it is hoped that if it proves acceptable, a larger work might be undertaken, in which case, I would indeed be very grateful to readers who could send me any points of interest or anecdotes about the breed, to Swainston Kennels, Startforth, Barnard Castle, Co. Durham.

As will be seen, I have given, where possible, various opinions of people on the breed at various dates, and I have taken a great many extracts from their works, which will be acknowledged when they are quoted; but, apart from this, I wish to express my particular thanks to the British Museum (Natural History Section) for the extreme courtesy and kindness they have always shown me, and the great trouble its members have put themselves to in supplying information. I also gratefully acknowledge help received from the Victoria and Albert Museum, the British Museum (the Department of British and Medieval Antiquities Section), H.M. Office of Works, the Royal College of Surgeons, the Zoological Society of London, and from the many correspondents who have been so kind as to reply to questions I have written to various papers.

1
Origin Theories

*"My lady, in her parlour snug,
Is still delighted with her pug."*
Joseph the Book Man, 1821

THE pug-dog has for many years been regarded as having sprung in some way or other from the bull-dog, and many of the older books on natural history dismiss him summarily with being "a bull-dog in miniature." The Lexiconists have mostly followed this example.

It is difficult to trace how and when this theory started, though it is probable that the similarity in appearance between the two breeds gave rise to it in the first place, despite the fact that when the pug-dog was first introduced in large numbers into England during the late seventeenth century, it was styled the Dutch Mastiff and not the Dutch Bull-Dog.

An examination of the skulls of a bull-dog and a pug dog shows clearly that, so far as anatomy goes, there is no relationship whatever between them.

The pug-dog appears undoubtedly to be a relation of the mastiff. Both mastiffs and pug-dogs were known at an early date in China, and the pug-dog, certainly, and possibly the mastiff, owe their origin to that country, though the latter was known very early in Europe.

Even today the standard British Museum catalogue[2] describes the pug-dog as having a possible relationship to the bulldog.

> "The Pug, which is believed to take its name from the Latin *pugnus,* a fist (in allusion to its short and square face), is evidently related to the Mastiff and the Bulldog, although this history of its descent is lost. It is believed, however, to have been originally produced in Holland, at a comparatively recent date. At any rate it was fashionable in that country in the time of King William III., by whom numerous specimens were brought to England, where the breed has ever since been popular. The Pug appears to have been always a fawn-coloured dog with a black face and curly tail; but about the middle of the nineteenth century two distinct strains—the Willoughby and the Morrison—were established. The former was characterised by the cold stone-fawn colour, and the excess of black, which showed itself in the completely or nearly black head and in the presence of a large 'saddle-mark' or wide 'traces.' The Morrison strain, on the other hand, had a richer and yellower fawn, with no extra blackness. The two strains are, however, now more or less completely blended. There is also a black breed, of very modern origin. Owing to the shortness of the jaws, the teeth of the Pug are crowded together, so much so that the premolar teeth frequently have their long diameter placed transversely instead of longitudinally. A similar feature often occurs in the skulls of Pekinese and Japanese Spaniels and other lap-dogs. The breed is represented by a specimen purchased in 1908."[3]

G. L. le Clerc Buffon, in his *Historie Naturelle,* published in 1750, who Rawdon B. Lee[4] describes as the most unreliable of naturalists and "whose word" according to "Stonehenge," "no man relies on," carries the bull-dog in miniature theory to even greater lengths when he describes how the bull-dog was imported into South Africa by the Hollanders, when the Cape was a Dutch settlement, where it became modified into the form of a pug-dog, and was reimported into Holland as a lady's pet!

The pug-dog and the bull-dog are, of course, entirely different in character, but the most decisive argument that can be brought against the theory of the pug-dog being a bull-dog in miniature is that the pug-dog is a very considerably older breed than the bull-dog, so far as historical traces go. "It has been suggested," writes Frederick Gresham,[5]

The "Doguin" from Buffon's *Historie Naturelle,* 1835 edition. From the Flamholtz collection.

> "that the Pug is of the same family as the Bull-dog, and that it was produced by a cross with this and some other smaller breed. But this is improbable, as there is reason to believe that the Pug is the older breed, and it is known that it has been bred with the Bull-dog for the anticipated benefit of the latter."

And the author of *The Sportsmans' Repository,* published in the early part of the nineteenth century, treats the matter in a lighter vein when he states:

> "Another, and which we deem an inconsequent conjecture on this most important affair of origination, is the Pug being, according to certain sage conjecturists, a sample or first-class mongrel, the production of a commixture between the English

Bull-dog and the little Dane, a conjecture we feel inclined to define by the figure *hysteron-proteron,* or setting the cart before the horse. We hold the Pug to be of the elder house; and if at this perilous anti-parodial crisis we may venture at a secular parody, the motto of the illustrious race of Pugs ought to be, not we from Bulls, but Bulls from us."

The pug-dog has been known by various classifications, but none of them seem to throw any light on its origin. It has generally been known as the *Canis fricator,* and some naturalists have classified it as being one of the four British dogs under the heading *Canis Anglicus,*[6] though it is more correctly classified under the *Pugnaces* group.

Edward C. Ash, in his *Dogs: Their History and Development,* published in 1927, states:

> "Dogs are members of that order of 'animals of prey' known as Carnivora, which with fifteen other orders, belong to a class of animals feeding their young by mammary glands, the Mammalia. The dogs . . . are, however, members of that easily distinguished family, the Canidae.
>
> "We find that the dog family . . . characterised on the whole by long and pointed muzzles except in some Eastern breeds such as the Japanese Spaniel, the Pug, and Pekinese....
>
> "If on the other hand domestic varieties have been bred from existing types of wolves, foxes and jackals, and have gradually . . . changed to what they are today, then we should get two or three marked races, the wolflike, foxlike and jackal-like; but

The Pug as pictured in the 1792 edition of Buffon's Histoire Naturelle, as published by Barr.

this would not explain the Thibet Mastiff or Bloodhound type or the shortfaced Pugs, Japanese Spaniels, unless their ancestral form of wild animal existed once and has died out."

This statement is extremely interesting, as it excludes the pug-dog from all other breeds except the Japanese Spaniel, the pekinese (or Pekin spaniel), the bloodhound and the mastiff.

One cannot help agreeing that the pug-dog and the mastiff are similar in every material respect except in that of size, and there seems no doubt that they are members of a similar group, or family, though it is difficult to say with any authority whether the mastiff[7] was bred from the pug-dog or the pug-dog from the mastiff. From the slight evidence there is before us it would appear that the pug-dog is the older breed. It must be remembered that all wild animals have a tendency to decrease in size and all domesticated animals to increase.

On the question of the bloodhound I would not like to express an opinion, but I cannot help feeling that the Pekin and Japanese spaniel are wrongly classified with the pug-dog and mastiff, because it would appear from their apple-shaped skulls that neither of them are naturally short-faced dogs. Both appear in the past to have had their faces considerably shortened by selective breeding, or inbreeding, resulting in the curious formation of their heads; and I suggest that both these species started out on life's journey with faces as long and pointed as the small old English spaniels exhibited at the present day, whereas an examination of the skulls will irrefutably show that those of pug-dog and mastiff are both of the same square character, totally in contradiction to the contracted appearance of the bull-dog's skull. It has been stated that the present-day pug-dog's face has been shortened by improved breeding. It must be clearly understood, however, that in-breeding was never necessary for this purpose. The pug-dog's muzzle, though longer in the past, has always been naturally square and inclined to shortness.

There can be no question that the muzzle of a dog can be shortened by selective breeding. The pug-dog is itself an example of this, though it has always been a naturally short-faced dog. In comparison with the skull of a short-faced spaniel the skull of a pug-dog or a mastiff is comparatively square and flat.

It seems quite clear, therefore, that our search for the origin of the pug-dog must commence where we find pug-dogs and mastiffs in conjunction. This was in China, from whence nearly all the short-faced breeds of dog sprang.

The strange depiction of the "Roquet," showing some Pug-like characteristics. From the 1835 edition of Buffon's *Histoire Naturelle.* **From the Flamholtz collection**

But before going so far as China there is one theory about the origin of the pug-dog which must be noted, because, though it has never, so far as I am aware, been stated in print, it is a theory often discussed and taken as correct. It is important in that it deals definitely with the first introduction of the breed into England.

Since the war—the exact date I have been unable to ascertain—a certain sale of china was held in London of various specimens, amongst which was a very old mother-of-pearl model of a short-faced, curly-tailed dog said to have been taken from an early Egyptian tomb.

In about 1888 certain alterations were made in the old Post Office in London, and during the excavation for a new site the foundations were sunk twenty-seven feet deeper, and an old Roman wall was discovered, together with the remains of a Roman villa, amongst which were found some animal remains, including the skull of a small, short-faced dog.

Upon these two statements is based a theory that the pug-dog was known to the ancient Egyptians, and during the period of Roman invasion of Egypt, specimens were imported into Rome as pets and from thence were imported into Britain—the first pug-dog, therefore, being introduced into this country some time during the period of Roman occupation. One might even carry this argument farther and suggest that the first pug-dogs were imported direct from Egypt by the Carthaginian traders, who are said to have brought across the mastiff.

I have been unable to trace anything with respect to the Egyptian dog, though it could not have been of such ancient lineage as some of the holders of this theory are inclined to believe, as mother-of-pearl was not, used by the ancient Egyptians in their modelling; and even during the Roman occupation of Egypt, when certain mosaic models were made, mother-of-pearl was rarely, if ever, used. I do not wish to deny the possibility of such a model having been discovered, possibly made of mother-of-pearl-like material, because where there is smoke there is usually fire, and the fact of the discovery being so often mentioned makes me think that there may be "something in it"; but without sufficient details being supplied to trace the actual specimen I would not like to express an opinion, except that this single model cannot be taken to be conclusive evidence that the pug-dog was known to the ancient Egyptians.

The Roman skull is certainly of greater interest, but again does not prove conclusive without further evidence to support it. I cannot trace this skull or I would supply a photograph in conjunction with the skulls of pug-dogs and other short-faced animals of the present day.

There seems little doubt, however, that such a skull was discovered,[8] and if the description given is accurate it would appear to have been that of a pug-dog as that was the only short-faced dog of the period. In a letter on the subject to the Zoological Society of London they informed me that:

> "There is no doubt, however, that it " (the pug-dog) " existed many years before the Romans invaded Britain, and there seems to be no reason why they should not have been responsible for introducing it into this country."

Roman ladies were known to cherish lap-dogs as pets, and pomeranians and dogs from the islands of Melita in the Aegean, now known as Maltese, were particularly favoured. General A. H. L. Fox Pitt-Rivers has also traced relics of turnspits, or dachshunds, as well as small retrievers. But apart from this single skull, no pug-dogs.

Again, I would like to say that the evidence is not strong enough to accept the theory of this skull being definitely established as that of a pug-dog, or that the breed was introduced into this country by way of Rome.

So far as England is concerned the pug-dog was unknown until the end of the seventeenth century, though James Watson in *The Dog Book,* published in 1906, is bold enough to state, without advancing any proof for his contention:

> "While we have credited Holland with the original possession of the pug, we are not prepared to advance any proof of the statement. Indeed, there is more reason, so far as the proofs we have seen, to suppose that it is every bit as much English as Dutch, but we need further information on the subject."

Apart from the Roman skull there seems to be only one other trace of the pug-dog in England prior to the Dutch invasion. Of this W. D. Drury, in his *British Dogs,* published in 1903, writes:

> "Coming to more recent times, we find the dearth of specific information with regard to dogs quite as great as that which characterised pre-mediæval days; while the representations of dogs upon monumental tombs are often so rude as to give but the slightest clue to the identity of the animals thereon depicted. Sometimes it is the Greyhound that is thus selected as an emblem of fidelity; at others a spotted dog, it may be a Dalmatian of the period, and at yet others a lap-dog, by some considered to represent a Pug of the period—namely, the latter part of the fourteenth century."

There seems to be only one other source from whence the pug-dog is claimed to have been imported—Muscovy, or Russia.

For many years the pug-dog has been a favourite in Russia. "There is yet," states *The Sportsman's Repository,*

> "an obscure but confident tradition, that Pugism had its origin in Muscovy; which, being granted, we may not have been wide of the mark in tracing in it the form of the Arctic dog."

And E. C. Ash, in his *Dogs and How to Know Them,* published in 1925, says that:

> "Hundreds of years ago Pug-dogs were a feature of the Moscow market; fine specimens sold at one shilling each. Varieties are fawns, also blacks and light creams. A black mask in fawns is an advantage.
>
> "Originating in China, this handsome toy-dog became very popular in England, and was kept by people of taste and refinement. A very old breed, likely to come popular again."

The theory that pug-dogs were imported from Russia is unquestionably correct. They were imported in large quantities from that country during the eighteenth and nineteenth centuries, but there is no trace of pug-dogs ever having been imported from Russia prior to the importation of pug-dogs from Holland.

Without further proof it is impossible to say that pug-dogs were known in this country before the seventeenth century, and we can therefore set out in our search for their origin, not as a bastard or in-bred bull-dog, but as an original species, in the country where there are the first traces of them—China.

The Pug

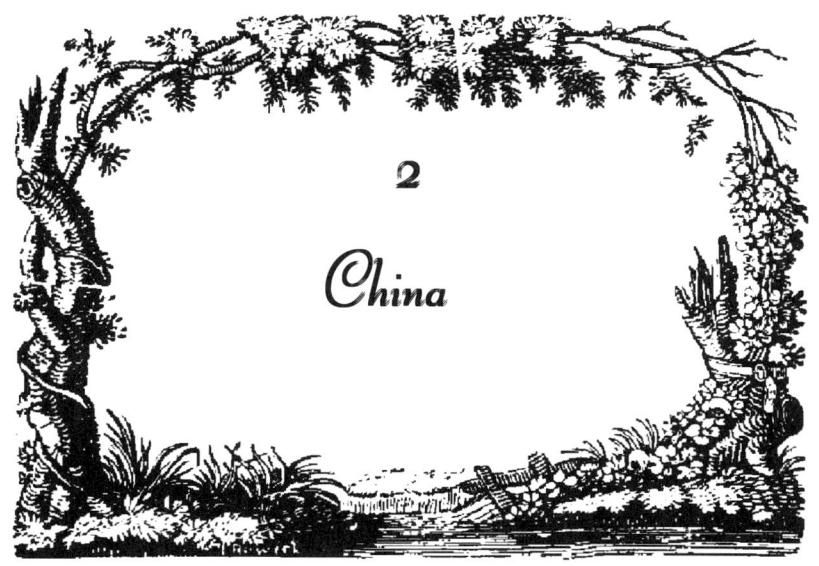

2
China

"A veritable pug of pugs, with large, soft, loving eyes."
The World, 1876

HE pug-dog was a well-known and well-authenticated Chinese breed of dog. It is said to have had its origin in a place in China called Lo-Chiang in the district of Ssuchuan, and the name given to it by the Chinese was *Lo-chiang-sze,* or, more simply, *Lo-sze.*[9]

It is difficult to state with any accuracy when the breed first came into prominence in China, but it was probably during the Chou dynasty, and, possibly, during the reign of the lascivious Yu-wang, who succeeded the warlike Suan-wang (827-782 B.C.).

According to the Zoological Society of London

> "the Pug-dog is known to be one of the oldest of breeds and originated in China some 700 years B.C."

whilst Edward C. Ash[10] states that

> "the breed probably originated in China, and spread from there to Japan, and thence to Europe. In China short-mouthed dogs known as 'Lo-sze' are mentioned in early native literature as far back as 700 B.C."

It is excessively difficult to say when the introduction of Chinese dogs into Japan commenced, but about A.D. 670 the Chinese and Japanese became interested in one another, and the Chinese presented the Japanese with small dogs which were regarded by the Japanese as being extremely valuable—so much so that when the Japanese Emperor demanded a tribute from China in A.D. 824, he included in his terms two Chinese *pai*[11] dogs as well as two of some other breed.

Again referring to Edward C. Ash, quoting from H. Ramsay's *Western Thibet,* published in 1890:

> "Chinese pug-dogs were also introduced as far as Lhasa. In Thibetan they were called *lags k'yi (i.e.* hand dogs), because it was believed that if a human being lays his hand upon a young eagle when freshly hatched, the bird is transformed into a dog of the Chinese pug breed."

It was not until about A.D. 100 that dogs in China were given individual names.

Another rather amusing anecdote is given by Edward C. Ash, but he does not state as to what breed of dog he refers:

> "From the official history of the Han dynasty (of A.D. 168-90) we learn that the Emperor Ling Ti was exceedingly interested in breeding dogs. To one kept in his western garden at Lo Yang (Honan-fu), he gave the official hat of the Chin Hsien grade, which, we read, was one of the most important literary ranks of the period. The hat was 8 3/4 inches high in front, 3 3/4 inches high behind, and 10 inches broad. Other dogs held other ranks, whilst females had the ranks to which wives of officials were entitled."

The Pekin spaniel probably sprang from the pug-dog by way of the short-coated Chinese Happa-dog. The Happa-dog is not well known in England, but there is an excellent stuffed specimen in the British Museum (Natural History Section), and it is not uncommon in the United States. Under the heading "Happa"

Shen Chen-Lin's drawing of a Chinese "Lo-Sze Dog."

in W. E. Mason's *Dogs of All Nations,* published in 1915, it is described as follows:

> "The Happa is identical in every respect with the Pekinese Spaniel, except that his coat is short and smooth."

One must be very careful not to confuse the Chinese Happa-dog with the Dutch *Happa-hond,* which is the term used in that country to describe a pug-dog.

Another confusion which arises over this Happa-dog is that, according to B. Laufer, there was in Turkey

> "a small and alert class" (of dog) "called *ha-pa* dogs."

It is difficult to say whether these Turkish *ha-pa* dogs were the same as Chinese Happa-dogs or a distinct breed altogether, or whether it was from Turkey, and not from China, that the pug-dog was imported, and the Dutch term of *Happa-hond* applied to the breed was merely another form of the Turkish *ha-pa.*

Toy-dogs appear to have become prominent in court circles during the Tang dynasty, according to the late Chinese minister, Lord Li Ching-fong, who wrote in *The Pekingese,* edited by Lillian C. Smythe:

The Chinese Happa Dog as it appeared in Mason's *Dogs of All Nations.*

"Toy dogs first became popular in the Tang Dynasty, that is, about the eighth century (Christian era), and again in the Sung Dynasty (eleventh century)."

Chinese legend tells us that the pekinese sprang from a mating between a marmoset and a lion, and though the dog, the Pekin spaniel, was common enough in China, certain specimens were kept in the royal palace and were regarded as sacred.

The Pekin spaniel was imported into Europe at an early date, and Mrs. Lilburn MacEwen in 1904 stated that they were known to the Court of Henri III., and came to the Court of our Charles II. Apparently they did not reach the United States until Mrs. Eva B. Guyer obtained a specimen from Europe in 1898.

The importation of the sacred Palace[12] dog did not take place till late in the nineteenth century. Lady Algernon Gordon-Lennox, writing in *Cassell's New Book of the Dog,* states that:

"The history of the breed in England dates from the importation in 1860 of five dogs taken from the Summer Palace, where they had, no doubt, been forgotten on the flight of the Court to the interior. Admiral Lord John Hay, who was present on active service, gives a graphic account of the finding of these little dogs in a part of the garden frequented by an aunt of the Emperor, who had committed suicide on the approach of the Allied Forces. Lord John and another naval officer, a cousin of the late Duchess of Richmond's, each secured two dogs; the fifth was taken by General Dunne, who presented it to Queen Victoria. Lord John took pains to ascertain that none had found their way into the French camp, and he heard then that the others had all been removed to Jehal with the Court. It is therefore reasonable to suppose that these five were the only Palace dogs, or Sacred Temple dogs of Pekin, which reached England, and it is from the pair which lived to a respectable old age at Goodwood that so many of the breed now in England trace their descent.

"Many years ago Mr. Alfred de Rothschild tried, through his agents in China, to secure a specimen of the Palace dog for the writer, in order to carry on the Goodwood strain, but without success, even after a correspondence with Pekin which lasted more than two years; but we succeeded in obtaining confirmation of what we had always understood: namely, that the Palace dogs are rigidly guarded, and that their theft is punishable by death. At the time of the Boxer Rebellion, only Spaniels, Pugs, and Poodles were found in the Imperial Palace when it was occupied by the Allied Forces, the little dogs having once more preceded the Court in the flight to Signanfu."

It will be seen from this account that pug-dogs were still kept as pets in the royal palace at Pekin as late as the end of last century.

No paintings or models of the pekinese type of dog, dating from earlier than the nineteenth[13] century, are known to exist.

Again referring to Edward C. Ash, I find that:

"There are considerable numbers of references to dogs in early chronicles. The Emperor Ren Tsung, about A.D. 1041, was faced by a mutiny of his palace troops. One of the officials (a censor) advised him that he ought to keep a dog. 'In Ssuchuan there is a place named Lochiang famous for its dogs. Search should be made for one of these having a red coat and a short tail. Such as these are very quick of ear and should be bred in the palace so as to give early warning of trouble outside.' The enemies of this censor, whose name was Sung, nicknamed him 'Sung Lo-chiang,'[14] for giving the Emperor this advice."

It is interesting to note that the pug-dog was even recognised in those days as being the best watch-dog—a title which he proved to be his with William of Orange, and one which every person knowing the breed will admit at the present day. With regard to the colour I can only suggest that there has been a mistake in the translation, or that the pug-dogs of that day were of a ruddier shade of fawn.

Dogs, both in China and Japan, were treated with an almost exaggerated consideration, and the smaller the breed the more highly it was prized. Kaempfer refers to dogs in Japan about 1727, when he tells how they

> "went by the place where publick orders and proclamations were put up, not far from the ditch of the castle, where we saw a new proclamation put up lately and twenty shuits of silver nail'd to the post to be given as a reward to any body that would discover the accomplice of a murder lately committed upon a dog."

In *A Journey to the Tea Countries of China,* by R. Fortune, published in 1852, a description is given of the toy-dogs of Japan:

"The lap-dogs of the country are highly prized both by natives and by foreigners. They are small—some of them not more than 9 or 10 inches in length. They are remarkable for sunk-noses and sunken eyes, and are cer-

A Chinese Lo-Sze, or Pug Dog, pictured in Peking, in 1914.

tainly more curious than beautiful. They are carefully bred; they command high prices even amongst the Japanese, and are dwarfed, it is said, by the use of saki—a spirit to which their owners are particularly partial. Like those of the larger breed already noticed, they are remarkable for the intense hatred they bear to foreigners."

G. R. Jesse, in his *Researches into the History of the British Dog,* published in 1866, refers to the above extract, and writes:

"The author expresses some surprise that the dogs share the antipathies of their masters. Does he not know that the animal is not only the most sincere, but the staunchest of friends? None can say of him: 'Out on this half-faced fellowship!' for our friends, are his friends; our enemies, his enemies."

The date of the first importation of pug-dogs from China or Japan direct to this country is lost, but certainly there was a good trade from China in pug-dogs during the early part of the nineteenth century, as the first Kennel Club Stud Book shows by entry: "Click, by Lamb (from Pekin) out of Moss."

The exaggerated pampering applied to toy-dogs in Japan resulted in the degeneration of the species. In China the dogs were treated with much more common sense. Edward Richard Lydekker, in his *Royal Natural History,* published in 1893, gives a description of a pug-dog imported from Japan:

"The Chinese, or, as it is often incorrectly called from being imported into Japan and thence brought to Europe, the Japanese pug, is a still more extraordinary animal, exhibiting a kind of degradation from over breeding. One of these brought to England about 1867 was a slender-legged animal with very long hair, and the bushy tail closely curled over its back. The face was extremely short, and the jaws very feeble, with only a single pair of incisor teeth in the lower one. This pug lived chiefly on vegetables and exhibited a special partiality for cucumber."

A detail from the painting of *Louis XIV with His Heirs,* by Largilliére.

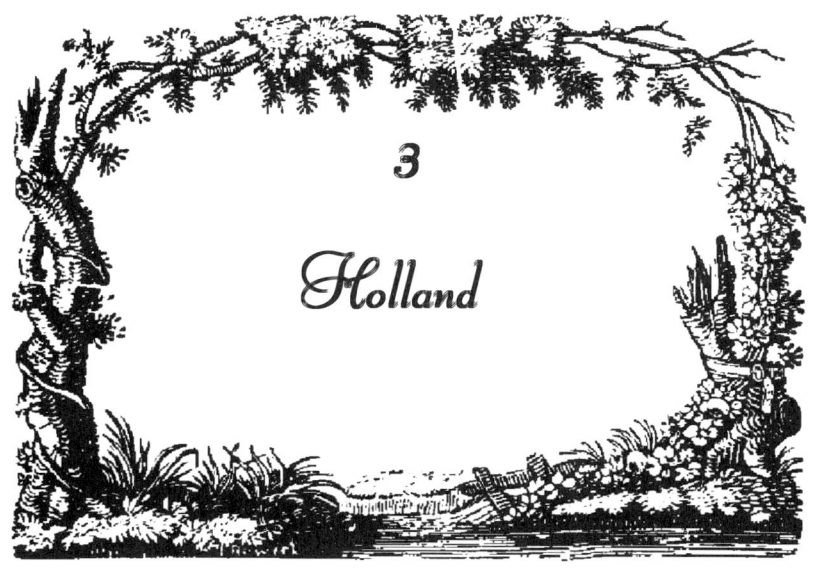

3
Holland

"Then half arose
His little pug-dog with his little pug-nose."
  R. H. Barham, Ingoldsby Legends, 1840

HE following query was inserted in *Notes and Queries,* second series, vol. v., on p. 131, for the year 1858. It received no replies:

"The Prince of Orange's Dog. Sir Roger Williams, in his *Actions of the Lowe Countries* (printed by Humfrey Lownes, for Mathew Lownes, 1618), 4to, p. 49, gives an interesting account of a Camisado, or night attack, by Julian Romero upon the camp of the Prince of Orange, in which the Prince's life was saved by a dog:

" 'For I heard the Prince say often, that as hee thought, but for a dog he had been taken. The Camisado was given with such resolution, that the place of armes tooke no alarme, untill their fellowes were running in with the enemies in their tailes. Whereupon this dogge, hearing a great noyse, fell to scratching and crying, and withall leapt on the Prince's face, awaking him being asleep, before any of his men. And albeit the Prince lay in his armes, with a lackey alwaies holding one of his horses ready bridled; yet at the going out of his tent, with much adoe hee recovered his horse before the enemie arrived. Nevertheless one of his Quiries was slaine taking horse presently after him; and divers of his servants were forced to escape amongst the guards of foote, which could not recover their horses. For truth, ever since, untill the Prince's dying day, he kept one of that dog's race; so did many of his friends and followers. The most or all of these dogs were white little hounds, with crooked noses, called Camuses.'

"The fashionable lap-dog of the days of the first two Georges was the ugly little Dutch pug. It was also customary to decorate them with orange-coloured ribbons.

"Query: Is the origin of this fashion to be traced to Sir Roger Williams' anecdote?

"EDWARD F. RIMBAULT."

To this query I answer "Yes."

In giving this answer I am treading on rather dangerous ground, for Captain A. H. Trapman has recently thrown a bombshell into the world of pugdom by describing the dog as a spaniel—a contention I have never heard before from a writer on canine matters.

Two historians of modern days have certainly described the dog to be a spaniel, but without giving any authority, and their statements have always been regarded, as far as I have heard, in the canine world as incorrect as to the breed of the dog; and every leading writer on dogs who has mentioned the incident has invariably given the palm for saving the Prince at Hermigny to the pug-dog. The result seems also to prove the contention, for the pug-dog was adopted as the favourite breed of the house of Orange from ever after the battle, and became widely popular throughout the whole of the Netherlands.

To give a careful consideration of the question it is necessary to set out several accounts of the battle. The most important, because it is the earliest and is written by a contemporary writer, is that of Sir Roger Williams, Kt., part of which has been set out in Mr. Rimbault's query:

"The Prince being retyred into his Campe, *Julian Romero* with earnest persuasions procured licence of Duke d'Alva, to hazard a Camisado that night upon the Prince. At midnight *Julian* sallyed out of the trenches with a thousand musketiers, and two thousand armed men, most pikes; all the rest stood in armes in the trenches, their horsemen ready without the trenches to second *Julian*, principally for his retreite if need were. *Julian* divided his forces into three troupes. The first two hundred olde

Carl Gustav Pilo's painting *The Ramel's Family Pug*

shot, which could keepe their matches close, led by a desperate Captain named *Muncheco*. The second one thousand armed men and shot, led by *Julian* himselfe. The third led by his Lieutenant Collonell and Sergeant Maior; whom he commanded to stand fast in the midst of their way betwixt the two Campes for his retriete; and not to stir unlesse some of credit came from him to Command the contrarie. Presently after his directions, he commanded *Muncheco* to charge; who resolutely forced two guards, being at the least a regiment of *Almaines*. *Julian* seconded with all resolution, in such sort, that hee forced all the guards that he found in his way into the place of armes before the Prince's tent. Here he entered divers tents; amongst the rest his men killed two of the Prince's secretaries hard by the Prince's tent, and the Prince himselfe escaped very narrowly."

Sir Roger's account continues in the words set out in Mr. Rimbault's query.

Ruth Putnam, the American historian, in his *William the Silent, Prince of Orange,* published in 1895, describes the action as follows:

"On the night of 11th September,[15] Julian Romero led a small force of six hundred men to Hermigny. The night was dark, and they had put their shirts out side of their armour to distinguish each other in the obscurity. Silently as snow they succeeded in surprising the sentinels, cutting them down like grass, and thus gained a way into the sleeping camp. Orange heard no noise, and slept quietly on until aroused by a little spaniel that was sleeping at his feet. Not content with barking, the little creature licked his master's face. The Prince sprang out of bed, seized a horse that was ready saddled, and rode off in the darkness."

The third account contains extracts from Motley, and is taken from the valuable book of Miss Estelle Ross, published in 1924 under the title of *The Book of Noble Dogs.*

"The Reformation, which the Earl of Wiltshire's dog hastened in England, was marked in Holland, then under Spanish yoke, by persecution. The Dutch patriots, of whom William, Prince of Orange, was leader, were reformers, and they headed a national rising against their oppressors.

"At one time the Spanish army was within half a league of Prince William's encampment at Hermigny, and the Spanish commander, Julian de Romero, determined on a surprise attack on the Dutch camp. Six hundred musketeers, their shirts over their armour to distinguish one another in the darkness, made a sortie and reached their objective without any alarm having been raised. 'The sentinels were cut down, the whole army surprised, while, for two hours long, from one o'clock in the morning till three, the Spaniards butchered their forces.'

"While this tumult was afoot, it is somewhat surprising that no sound roused the Prince of Orange and his attendants. One alone awoke to the danger—the little pug-dog Pompey, who slept on his bed. 'This creature,' Motley writes in *The Rise of the Dutch Republic,* 'sprang forward at the sound of hostile footsteps, and scratched his master's face with his paws. There was but just time for the Prince to mount a horse, which was ready saddled, and to effect his escape through the darkness before his enemies sprang into the tent. His servants were cut down, the master of his horse, and two of his secretaries, who gained their saddles a moment later, all lost their lives, and but for the little dog's watchfulness, William of Orange, upon whose shoulders the whole weight of his country's fortunes depended, would have been led within a week to an ignominious death.'

"The Prince himself frequently acknowledged his indebtedness: 'but for my little dog I should have been killed.'

"There is doubt whether Pompey perished that day, or whether, as Freville, with what authority we cannot trace, states, he lived and was a second time instrumental in saving his master's life, remaining with him till its close, when he defied the undertaker's men to lay the body in the coffin.

"One thing is certain: from that day forward the Prince was never without a pug sleeping on his bed; and where he sleeps in effigy in Delft Cathedral one lies at his feet.

"When William III. came to the throne of England, Dutch pugs, decked with yellow ribbons, became fashionable pets in honour of the house of Orange."

Both Motley and Putnam describe the dog as a spaniel (sic); but both are modern historians, not writers on canine matters, and breeds of dogs were very confused in the sixteenth century. I would prefer to rely on the description given by Sir Roger. The word *Camus* is French, and means "flat-nosed." Gilpin, R.A., as early as 1798, described them as "Dutch Pugs."

Spaniels were a well-known breed in England at that date, though there were certainly no shortfaced varieties. The name, of course, comes from "Espaignol," meaning Spanish, and the breed was referred to in England as far back as Chaucer.[16] It is remarkable, therefore, that if Sir Roger meant a spaniel he should not have said a spaniel. He is apparently at a loss to describe this new specimen of the canine species, and he merely calls it the "white 'flat-nosed.' " The word "white" can be taken to mean light of colour.

Idstone (the Rev. T. Pearce) bears out these theories in his book, *The Dog,* published in 1872:

"The Pug was most fashionable about 1702, and especially from the time of William III. to George II. He was decorated with orange ribbons; and the reasons for William's partiality to the breed are given in a scarce book called *Sir Roger Williams: His Actions of the Low Countries* (1618). This book states: 'The Prince of Orange being retired into camp, Julian Romero procured the licence of the Duke of D'Alva to hazard a camisado or night attack on the prince. Julian sallied out with a thousand pikemen, found their way to the prince's tent, and killed two of his secretaries. The prince's dog fell to scratching, and awakened him: and ever after the prince kept a dog of the breed. They are not remarkable for their beauty, being little white dogs, with crooked, flat noses, called "Camuses" —Camus meaning "flatnosed." ' Gilpin, R.A., in 1798, called them 'Dutch Pugs.' I have no doubt that the 'white' dogs mentioned above were drab or granite-coloured dogs of a light tint."

Rawdon B. Lee, too, gives the story, and states that:

> "History tells us that the pug became first favourite at the Dutch Court,"

after the incident which he describes in terms very similar to those quoted above; and, again, Edward C. Ash and V. W. F. Collier[17] follow his example.

I have myself heard the pug-dog referred to in Germany as "The Lutherean dog," because, by this incident, it was said to have been the cause of the continuance of the reformation in Europe; and the Church of England certainly owes its existence to the pug-dog for, had the house of Orange failed, there would have been no Protestant champion to take over the throne after England had relapsed under James II.

The arms of our bishops should be supported by a pug-dog on one side and a spaniel on the other, for it was certainly a spaniel belonging to Lord Wiltshire which was, according to Foxe, one of the chief causes of the breach of this country with Rome.

There seems to me to be no possibility of doubt that it was a pug-dog which saved William of Orange.

But in the first place, how did the pug-dog get to Holland?

The Portuguese and Spaniards were trading with the East during the early part of the sixteenth century, but the Dutch certainly were not.

The battle of Hermigny was fought in 1572, and pug-dogs must have been in Holland before that time. Now the *Oostindische Vereenigde Maatschappij,* which was afterwards known as the Dutch East India Company, was not formed until the 20th of March 1602, so all the statements that have so often been made to the effect that it was this company which imported the pug-dog are erroneous. In fact, no Dutch ship sailed to the East before the 2nd of April 1595, when an expedition set out under Cornelius Houtman. However, before the union between Spain and Portugal in 1580 the Dutch had been the chief carriers of Eastern produce from Lisbon to Northern Europe, and it is probable that the first pug-dogs were brought from China by the Spanish, or, more probably, Portuguese ships, about the beginning of the sixteenth century; and the dogs were then purchased by the Dutch sailors and reshipped to Holland, by whom they were, apparently, at first named *Camuses,* because of their peculiar appearance, and, later, *happa-honds.*

William of Orange was, no doubt, presented with one of these new arrivals by his sailors, which he called Pompey; and after the battle of Hermigny they immediately became popular, not only with the Court, but with the whole people of Holland.

This is rather remarkable, as there seems to be no records of pug-dogs being known in Spain during the sixteenth century. There was certainly one theory I heard which connected the pug-dog with the Spanish Court. It has been said that the pug-dog was popular at the Court of Ferdinand and Isabella, and that because of this they were known as "Isabelleans," which explains the fact that many of the early female specimens of the breed were named Bella, just as many of the male specimens were called Pompey. I cannot trace any proof that the pug-dog was known to the Court of Ferdinand and Isabella, and I believe the name Isabelleans arose from a very different source.

In France fawn colour is known as Isabelle—the colour so called is the yellow of soiled calico.[18] The word arose from a vow made by Isabel of Austria (d. 1633), daughter of Philip II. of Spain, at the siege of Ostend, not to change her linen till the fort was captured. The siege lasted three years! A similar story is told of Isabella of Castile at the siege of Granada. This may possibly explain the term "Isabellean" being applied to pug-dogs at a time when the black variety were unknown.

William III. of Nassau, Prince of Orange, posthumous son of William II., Prince of Orange, and of Mary, daughter of Charles I. of England, grandson of William I., Prince of Orange, who was saved by his pug-dog Pompey, was born in 1650. He married

Mary, eldest daughter of James II. of England, and succeeded to the stadtholdership of the Netherlands in 1672. He landed at Torbay in England on the 5th November 1688, and was crowned as William III. on the 11th of April 1689. And with him when he landed were his *happa-honds,* which came over from Holland in large numbers as part and parcel of his retinue.

Thus, late in the year 1688, the first known contingent of pug-dogs honoured this country with their arrival.

I cannot omit a reference to the somewhat vexed question of the pug-dog in Dutch art. There are a considerable number of Dutch pictures containing pug-dogs, and also Dutch ware, particularly mugs, was often decorated with a pug-dog's head.

"Many an old Dutch jug," writes E. C. Ash in his *Dogs and How to Know Them,*

> "shows strange and often grotesque specimens of the Pug-dog, dancing on its hind legs to music."

James Watson, mentioning the subject, states that:

> "In the Bloomfield Moore collection of pottery in Centennial Hall, Philadelphia, we saw a good many years ago a cropped pug with two puppies in Delft ware, which was dated as seventeenth-century production; but on making inquiry regarding it, for the purpose of illustration, investigation was made, and it was found that the date given was wrong, and it is not believed to be over one hundred years old."

Mr. Watson, in his interesting article on pug-dogs in early Dutch art, failed to find in the New York collection any early picture or ware containing representation of pug-dogs. These early paintings and ware illustrated by Dutch pug-dogs are so often referred to, that when I noticed the following sentence:

> "In many of the paintings of the old Dutch and Flemish masters, dogs of unmistakable Pug type may be seen as accessories in pictures of domestic life."

in an article by Mr. Robert Leighton in *The Dog World,* for the 8th of February 1929, I asked my husband to write to *The Dog World,* so that we might have the opinion of this established authority on the question, and Mr. Leighton very kindly replied in the same paper on the 22nd of February 1929, as follows:

"THE DOG IN ART

"Referring to my article on the origin of the Pug, which appeared in *The Dog World* of 8th February, Mr. C. J. S. Goodger asks me to state definitely the name of any Dutch paintings in which the Pug is represented. I am afraid I cannot supply him with precise information concerning individual pictures; but it is a habit of mine, when visiting Continental art galleries, to make note of early paintings in which dogs of recognisable breed are introduced, and I have come upon several such paintings representing small dogs of Pug type in the galleries of Brussels, Amsterdam, The Hague, and Copenhagen.

"I especially remember one by Gabriel Metzu (1630-1667) in the Hermitage collection at Petrograd, in which an unmistakable Pug is very accurately treated by an artist, who evidently understood the characteristics of the breed. From this circumstance it is to be judged that the Pug was a familiar breed in Holland durmg the seventeenth century, and probably earlier.

"I regret that I cannot particularise, but I do not preserve my notes or keep the catalogues after they have served their purpose of helping me to trace the history of the different canine breeds. I can only assure Mr. Goodger that my statement was not made at random. The old Flemish and Dutch masters were very fond of introducing dogs as accessories in their pictures of domestic life, as any one may realise who visits the loan collection of Dutch art now being exhibited at Burlington House."

4
17th and 18th Century England

"A fine lady...keeps a Pug-dog, and hates the Parsons."
D. Garrick: Lethe, 1749

URING the Tudor period in England pet dogs were not generally cultivated, people being more partial to the larger breeds of hunting dogs; whilst, as ever in England, the oldest British breed of dog, the mastiff, was widely kept. In the reign of Henry VIII. strict laws were passed, forbidding dogs being brought to Court, so that his palaces might be

> "swete, wholesome, cleane, and well furnished as to a prince's house and state doth apertyne."

Henry himself, however, was above his laws, and had great partiality for his two dogs, Cutte and Belle, and also, it is said, for the two turnspits of his palace, Hob and Nob. Spaniels, too, were popular during this reign, the most famous being that belonging to the Earl of Wiltshire, which was hacked to death by the Swiss Guard in the Vatican.[19]

James V. of Scotland, Henry's contemporary, showed great favour for his hunting dogs, Basche and Bawtie, and every one knows the story of the fidelity of the little spaniel[20] belonging to his ill-fated daughter, Mary, Queen of Scots.

Mary's son, who ascended the throne of England under the title of James I., inherited his mother's love for dogs—though, again, his affection was for dogs of a large breed, and particularly for his dog named Jewell, who was accidentally shot by his queen. His son, Charles I., divided his affection between his greyhound Gipsey and Prince Rupert's white poodle, Boye, who lost his life at Marston Moor. In this reign it was said that greyhounds were the kings of dogs, spaniels were gentlemen and hounds but yeomen. It was, of course, before the arrival in Britain of the pug-dog, because, if he had been there at this time, I am sure he would have been the emperor of dogs.

Charles II., as all the world knows, went in entirely—after the Restoration—for the toy spaniels which bear his name, whilst James II. is said not to have scrupled to sacrifice the lives of his sailors to save his favourite dog, Mumper.

In these reigns the fashions of the people chiefly followed those set by their sovereigns.

But from the time of the Stuart accession dogs were not the only animals kept as pets, and, particularly in the reign of the second Charles, monkeys, which were then called pugs, vied with the small dogs for the favour of the great ladies of the land. Notices frequently appeared in the news-sheets of the time, such as: "Lady So-and-so was seen in the Mall followed by her page carrying her pug."

The word "pug" is of considerable antiquity in England, and is derived from the word "puck" meaning an "imp" or "fairy." In early days it was used purely as a term of endearment:

> "If in a couche, a fyne fleesde lambe a kinge shoulde cause to ryde. And geve it rayments neate and gay and call it pugges and prety peate."
>
> T. DRANT, 1566.

"My sweete pugge . . . thi absens will make the returne of thy swete cumpany the more welcum to me."
Sir G. CAREY, 1580.

"I have had foure husbands my selfe. The first, I called, sweet duck: the second, deare heart, the third, prettie pugge."
ANTONIO's *Revenge,* 1602.

"My prettie Pug (so fooles, hugging their bables, tearme them)."
RANDLE COTGRAVE, 1611.

About the time of the accession of the house of Stuart, the word "pug" used as a term of endearment seems to have gone out of fashion, and was applied as a name to the small monkeys that were then being imported. I have little doubt that the word was the same as that used as a term of endearment and was not, as has so often been stated, a new word coined from the Latin *pugnus* (meaning "a fist"), taken from the fact that the shadow of a pug's head on a wall resembled a clenched fist.

All the following quotations, which have over and over again been quoted in proof of the early arrival of pug-dogs in this country, do not refer to pug-dogs but to pugs:

"A little puppie, or pug to play with."
RANDLE COTGRAVE, 1611.

"Pugs and Baboons may claim a Traduction from Adam as well as these."
H. POWER, 1664.

"As if he had sent his Lady Apess with a puglet or two to have squeal'd and scream'd at us."
T. FLATMAN, 1681.

"The monkey by chance came jumping out with them.... Poor Pug was had before his betters."

J. CRULL, 1698.

"Poor Pug was caught, to town conveyed. There sold. How envied was his doom. Made captive in a lady's room."

J. GAY.

—whilst the word "pug," used by Ben Jonson in "The Devil is an Ass" in 1616, and the following quotation from Samuel Butler in 1664 refers to the word "pug" in its pure meaning of "puck," an imp or fairy:

"AGRIPPA'S PUG

"Quoth Hudibras—
Agrippa kept a Stygian pug
I' th' garb and habit of a dog,
That was his tutor, and the cur
Read to th' occult philosopher,
And taught him subtly to maintain
All other sciences are vain "

All these proofs that the pug-dog was known in England before the reign of William III. whittle away when the full texts are considered.

As a matter of fact, the earliest English reference to the pug-dog in print that I can trace does not appear to be before Bailey wrote, Pug, *a Nickname for a Monkey or Dog*, in 1731; and even as late as the time of Samuel Johnson, the word "pug" is referred to as meaning a monkey, and the word "pug-dog" is not mentioned:

"*Pug*.—A kind name of a monkey, or any thing tenderly loved. ('Upon setting him down, and calling him *pug*, I found him to be her favourite monkey.'—ADDISON.)" [21]

Idstone furnishes a different theory altogether and takes the name from the Greek:

> "I have stated, in an article written by me for the *Field Newspaper,*" he writes, "that this dog derives its name from a Greek word...whence comes the Latin *pugnus,* a fist,' because the shadow of a clenched fist was considered to resemble the dog's profile."

This theory of Idstone was attacked by Hugh Dalziel in his *British Dogs,* published in 1888, with, I think, some effect; but I cannot accept his suggestion set out at the end of the quotation.

> "As to the origin of the name, 'Idstone'—a writer always prone to travel miles out of the way to drag in a fanciful or obscure word or meaning, rather than use the commonplace one that stares everybody in the face—says"

A print by J. Greenaway. From the Flamholtz collection.

He gives the quotation set out above, and continues:

> "I call that learned nonsense, because there is not a vestige of proof advanced, or to be advanced, in support of it. It would have been a more reasonable suggestion that the dog was named Pug because of being short and thick set."

Pug-dogs immediately came into popularity with the accession of William III., and, as they rose in favour, so did the pugs sink, and finally disappeared. The new breed on its introduction was called Dutch Mastiffs or, more commonly, Dutch Pugs, because their wrinkled masks were thought to resemble the faces of the pugs of the day. When the pugs ceased altogether to be fashionable, the prefix "Dutch" was dropped, and the breed began to be called simply "pugs," or, more correctly, "pug-dogs."

The dogs of this time were light fawns, rather larger in size than those bred at present, with dark masks, a more clearly defined trace, and certainly longer in the face than those which would be accepted nowadays. Their tails were tightly curled and their ears cropped close to the head. I have been unable to ascertain when cropping the ears commenced, but this disfigurement continued to be seen up to the present century, despite the protests of Idstone in 1872.

> "In the old days it would have been impossible to have found a good specimen uncropped, but the remonstrances of judges and purchasers had their effect, and all the best dogs shown had their ears as nature made them, until the exhibition of 1871, at the Crystal Palace, where, I regret to say, several mutilated specimens were exhibited.
>
> "The reason assigned for thus disfiguring them is an exceedingly weak one, that it, 'adds to the puckers or wrinkles in the forehead': but this is not true; in fact, it has a tendency to draw the skin of the forehead tight. I would never myself give a prize to any Pug-dog thus tor-

tured if there were one unmutilated in the class which could be called a fair example; and I trust that all judges will discountenance the exercise of these barbarous customs."

Some extraordinary views were held as to the requisites of the pug-dog when it was first introduced into this country, amongst which was the belief that the tongue should protrude from the mouth—a blemish which we now know to be caused through partial paralysis of that organ. Another was that the tails of female pug-dogs were not considered correct unless they were curled on the opposite side of the back to those of a male.[22]

> "About the time Hogarth, the great painter, flourished," writes Rawdon B. Lee, "Dutch pugs were as fashionable as black pages, and no lady of title was considered to be fully equipped unless she had both in her following."

The sudden popularity of the new breed and its curious appearance immediately excited the caricaturists of the time, who were particularly prolific during the days of the Georges, and especially during the rebellions of 1715 and 1745; and the great people of the land, who nearly all kept pug-dogs, were continually finding themselves caricatured with pug-dog faces.

J. G. Wood, in his *Illustrated Natural History,* published in 1851, writes concerning him:

> "The Pug-dog is an example of the fluctuating state of fashion and its votaries. Many years ago the Pug was in a very great request as a lap-dog or 'toy' dog, as these little animals are more correctly termed. The satirical publications of the last century are full of sarcastic remarks upon Pug-dogs and their owners, and delighted in the easy task of drawing a parallel between the black-visaged, dumpy-muzzled dog, and the presumed personal attractions of its owner.'

A porcelain depiction, made about 1750, taken from the mold of the sculptor Roubillac. He modeled Hogarth's beloved dog Trump. Many authorities believe that Trump was a Pug cross and that earlier Hogarth pet Pugs were far more typical of the breed.

Foremost among the artists of the day was William Hogarth, a stalwart fancier of the breed, and his inseparable companion was his pug-dog, Trump, whom he has immortalised in a painting, which now hangs in the Tate Gallery, of himself and his dog. On its first exhibition it elicited a satire on the two

"Insep'rate companions! and, therefore, you see,
Cheek by jowl they are drawn in familiar degree "

This famous portrait, executed in 1749, was, according to Frederick W. Peel in his *Hogarth and His House,* at first hung in the National Gallery.

Some of Hogarth's other drawings gave offence, and he was himself subject to the venom of his fellow caricaturists. He was given the name of "Painter Pugg," and in two prints issued in 1753 and 1754 he is depicted with the lower half of his figure being in the form of a pug-dog, whilst one of these prints contains a representation of a pug-dog at the top of the picture.

"The word of professional scoffers and virtuosi,"

writes Austin Dobson, in his *William Hogarth,* published in 1902:

"fell joyously upon its obscurities and incoherencies while the caricaturists diverted themselves hugely with fancy representations of 'Painter Pugg.'"

"Dunce connoisseurs extol the author Pug,
The senseless, tasteless, impudent hum-bug"

Roubillac, the sculptor, was a friend of Hogarth, and not only modelled the bust of Hogarth, which is now in the National Portrait Gallery, but also modelled the pug-dog Trump.

These satires upon the breed and its owners did not affect its general popularity, and David Garrick (1716-79) ridiculed the prevailing fashion in his *Lethe*.

Edward C. Ash gives the following amusing advertisement in his chapter on pug-dogs as relating to the breed, and though the dog required is described as a lap-spaniel of uncertain colour, the description leaves no doubt as to Mrs. Smith wanting a pug-dog. The advertisement was inserted in the *Daily Advertiser,* in November 1744:

"An Exceeding small Lap Spaniel. Any one that has (to dispose of) such a one, either dog or bitch, and of any colour or colours, that is very, very small, with a very *short round snub nose,* and good ears.[23]

"If they will bring it to Mrs. Smith, at a coachmaker's over against the Golden Head, in Great Queen Street, near Lincoln's Inn Fields, they may (if approved of) have a very good purchaser. And to prevent any farther trouble: If it is not exceeding *small* and has anything of a longish peaked nose, it will not at all do. And nevertheless, after this advertisement is published no more, If any person should have a little creature, that answers the character of the advertisement, If they will please but to remember the direction, and bring it to Mrs. Smith, the person is not *so* provided, but that such a one will still at any time be, hereafter, purchased."

It makes one wonder what price was charged in those days per line for an advertisement!

The breed always had royal favour during the time of the first two Georges, but it was on the marriage of George III. to Princess Charlotte of Mecklenburg Strelitz on the 8th September 1761, that they reached the height of popularity. Charlotte was a passionate pug-dog lover, and was never without one or more round her, and the love of her husband for the breed has been kept for us by the portrait, which hangs at Hampton Court, of himself with his pug-dog.

Towards the end of the eighteenth century the unrest abroad, followed by wars on the Continent, caused a distinct decrease in the demand for pet dogs; and though George IV. is said to have kept a pug-dog, neither the pug-dog nor any other breed of dogs seems to have been prominent, despite the fact that Professor Gmelin had discovered three new forms of pug-dog—the Alicant,[24] the Artois and the bastard pug-dog, the latter of which he describes:

> "Bastard Pug-Dog. *Canis hybridus.* Has small, half pendulous ears, and a thick flatish nose."

Not much of a description, I am afraid. The following are the classifications of pug-dog as set out by him in his *Animal Kingdom,* translated by Robert Kerr, and published in 1792:

> "Pug-dog. *Canis fricator.* The nose is crooked upwards, the ears are pendulous, and the body square built.
>
> "This variety has a resemblance to the bull-dog, but is much smaller and entirely wants his savage ferocity. Of this there are two sub-varieties, viz.:
>
> "(a) The Artois dog, of Buffon, produced between the pug-dog and bastard pug-dog.

"(b) The Alicant dog, of Buffon, produced between the pug-dog and Spaniel."

It is rather interesting to consider for a moment as to how pet dogs were treated during this century. Great changes in their treatment had taken place since Dame Juliana Berners, Prioress of St. Albans, wrote in the fifteenth century of "smalle ladye's poppees that bere awaye the flees." Dame Juliana, it is interesting to note, was the first British authoress.

A description of the life of a lap-dog is very clearly set out in the first work of canine fiction, *The History of Pompey the Little, or The Life and Adventures of a Lapdog*, by Francis Coventry, and published in 1751. This book ran through many editions and was very popular in its day, Lowndes describing it as "an admirable *jeu d'esprit.*" From the frontispiece to my copy (1773, fifth edition) Pompey would appear to be a type of small spaniel, but the adventures of his life would apply equally well to a pug-dog, as his mistress, "Lady Tempest," also kept with him

"an Italian greyhound, a Dutch pug, two black spaniels of King Charles's breed, a harlequin greyhound, a spotted Dane and a mouse-coloured English bull-dog "

The meeting of these dogs with their new companion, Pompey, which also includes a description of how lapdogs were fed in those days, is set out as follows:

"They heard their mistress's rap at the door, and were assembled in the dining-room, ready to receive her: but on the appearance of master Pompey, they set up a general bark, perhaps out of envy; and some of them treated the little stranger with rather more rudeness than was consistent with dogs of their education. However, the lady soon interposed her authority, and commanded silence among them, by ringing a little bell, which she kept by her for that purpose. They all obeyed the signal instantly, and were still in a moment; upon which she carried little Pompey round, and obliged them all to salute their new acquaintance, at the same time commanding some of them to ask pardon for their unpolite behaviour; which whether they understood or not, must be left to the reader's determination. She then summoned a servant, and ordered a chicken to be roasted for him; but hearing that dinner was just ready to be served up, she was pleased to say, he must be contented with what was provided for herself that day, but gave orders to the cook to get ready a chicken to his own share against night.

"Her ladyship now sat down to table, and Pompey was placed at her elbow, where he received many dainty bits from her fair hands, and was caressed by her all dinner-time, with more than usual fondness."

The agreement for mating Pompey with a dog belonging to a Mrs. Racket was entered into by an exchange of the following two letters:

"DEAR TEMPEST,—MY favourite little Veny is at present troubled with certain amorous infirmities of nature, and would not be displeased with the addresses of a lover. Be so good therefore to send little Pompey by my servant who brings this note, for I fancy it will make a very pretty breed, and when the lovers have transacted their affairs, he shall be sent home incontinently.—Believe me, dear Tempest, yours affectionately,
RACKET."

"DEAR RACKET,—Infirmities of nature we all are subject to, and therefore I have sent master Pompey to wait upon miss Veny, begging the favour of you to return him as soon as his gallantries are over. Consider, my dear, no modern love can, in the nature of things, last above three days, and therefore I hope to see my little friend again very soon.—Your affectionate friend,
TEMPEST."

Cruelty was rife, and parents, apparently, made no endeavours to prevent their children treating their pets in the most inhuman manner possible.

"To say the truth, he soon began to find himself very unhappily situated in this family; for wretched are those animals that become the favourites of children. At first indeed he suffered only the barbarity of their kind-

This superb drawing is from Rev. J. G. Wood's *Animate Creation.*

ness, and was persecuted with no other cruelties than what arose from their extravagant love of him; but when the date of his favour began to expire (and it did not continue long) he was then taught to feel how much severer their hate could be than their fondness. He had indeed, from the first, two or three dreadful presages of what might happen to him; for he had seen with his own eyes the two kittens, his playfellows, drowned for some misdemeanor they had been guilty of, and the magpye's head chopt off with the greatest passion, for daring to peck a piece of plumb-cake that lay in the window without permission; which instances of cruelty were sufficient to warn him, if he had any foresight, of what might afterwards happen to himself.

"But he was not long left to entertain himself with conjectures, before he felt in person and in reality the mischievous disposition of these little tyrants. Sometimes they took it into their heads that he was full of fleas, and then he was soused into a tub of water till he was almost dead, in order to kill the vermin that inhabited the hair of his body. At other times he was set on his hinder legs with a book before his eyes, and ordered to read his lesson; which not being able to perform, they whipped him till he howled, and then chastised him the more for daring to be sensible of pain."

In those days, before the lethal chamber had been invented, the usual method of destroying a dog appears to have been by hanging: "She rang her bell instantly with the greatest fury, and on the appearance of a footman, ordered him" (the dog) "immediately to be hanged."

If one desires a complete view of the life of a lap-dog during the eighteenth century, the book should be read in full, and it well repays the time spent on it; but it will be sufficient for our purpose if the above extracts give a rough idea of the position in life occupied by a lap-dog at this period in our history.

5

France and Italy

"You'll be thinking of keeping pug-dogs and parrots next."
D. Jerrold, 1851

OT only in England did the pug-dog become popular, but abroad, particularly in Holland, France and Italy. He does not appear to have been really popular in Germany till a later date, though there are traces of him during the eighteenth century in that country.

It is possible that his popularity in Italy started through the introduction of "Punchinello," from the Levant, by Silvio Forillo, about the beginning of the seventeenth century, at Naples; and the most suitable dog found for the part of Toby was generally a pug-dog—not a poodle, which one would have expected, as poodles were up to that time believed to be the most intelligent dogs for stage work. Probably the pug-dog, on his introduction, appeared the more comical of the two. Certainly, when "Punchinello" reached this country, under the name of "Punch and Judy," during the reign of William III., the part of Toby was always taken by a pug-dog.

Charles Dickens, in his *Shy Neighbours,* mentions two such Tobys:

> "I never saw either guilty of the falsehood of failing to look down at the man inside the show, during the whole performance. The difficulty other dogs have in satisfying their minds about these dogs, appears to be never overcome by time. The same dogs must encounter them over and over again as they trudge along in their off minutes behind the legs, and beside the drum, but all dogs seem to suspect their frills and jackets."

But he could never be taken as a lover of the breed; probably he never possessed one. His description of the pug-dog was almost as terrible as that of Washington Irving. I give the description by Dickens from Miss Estelle Ross:

> "The novelist tells us that one of his earliest recollections was of a pug-dog, which he met daily on his way to school. It was puffy, 'black-muzzled, with white teeth and crisp curling tail, with a rooted animosity to little boys, barking at them and snapping at their bare legs.... From an otherwise unaccountable association of him with a fiddle, we concluded that he was of French extraction and his name Fidele. He belonged to some female, chiefly inhabiting a back parlour, whose life appears to have been consumed in sniffing and wearing a black beaver bonnet.' "

Washington Irving's description is even worse:

> "A little, old, grey-muzzled curmudgeon, with an unhappy eye, that kindles like a coal, if you only look at him; his nose turns up, his mouth is drawn into wrinkles so as to show his teeth; in short, he has altogether the look of a dog far gone in misanthropy, and totally sick of the world. When he walks, he has his tail curled up so

A print of the painting "Protection," by Sperling, 1892.

tight, that it seems to lift his feet from the ground. This wretch is called Beauty."

But we are getting away from the Continent towards the United States, and we will return to Italy with Mrs. Hester Piozzi on her tour of that country in 1786:

> "A transplanted Hollander, carried thither originally from China, seems to thrive particularly well in this part of the world; the little pug-dog, or Dutch mastiff, which our English ladies were once so fond of, that poor Garrick thought it worth his while to ridicule them for it in the famous dramatic satire called 'Lethe,' has quitted London for Padua, I perceive; where he is restored happily to his former honours, and every carriage I meet has a pug in it. That breed of dogs is now so near expired among us, that I recollect only Lord Penryn who possesses such an animal."

She found that pug-dogs, as well as other small breeds, were treated with an exaggerated kindness and consideration in Italy.

"A very veracious man"

informed her, she writes,

> "yester morning, that his poor wife was half brokenhearted at hearing such a Countess's dog was run over; 'for,' said he, 'having suckled the pretty creature herself, she loved it like one of her children.' I bid him repeat the circumstance, that no mistake might be made; he did so; but seeing me look shocked, or ashamed, or something he did not like, 'Why, Madam,' said the fellow, 'it is a common thing enough for ordinary men's wives to suckle the lap-dogs of ladies of quality'; adding that they were paid for their milk, and he saw no harm in gratifying one's *superiors*. As I was disposed to see nothing but harm in disputing with such a competitor, our conference finished soon; but the fact is certain."

Thomas Bewick (1753-1828), in his *History of Quadrupeds,* also bears out the affection of the Ladies of Italy for the pug-dog and claims that

> "it still maintains its place in the favour of the fair ones of that country."

Buffon shows clearly the popularity of the pug-dog in France at his day and he gives two names to the breed, which he calls *Le Doguin ou Mopse.* These two names are rather curious. "Le Doguin" approximately means the small *dogue* (bull-dog), and "Mopse" being a derivation, I presume, of the German name for the breed, *Mopshund.*

Idstone, dealing with this question of foreign names, states:

> "That their jet-black muzzle obtained for them the name of *carlins,* from the famous Parisian Harlequin, but they were previously known as *Doguins,* or *Roquets,* though now they are known as Pugs in France and Italy. The name Carlin is interesting, as proving that the black mask was valued in France; though it was either overlooked, or they did not take the trouble to attain it, in Italy."

As a matter of fact, *Carlin* is the common name for the breed at the present day in France, and the name given to it in Italy is *Cagnuolo.*[25]

But perhaps the greatest of pug-dog lovers of all time was to be found in France. This was Madame Josephine Beauhaernais, who was never without one, even during the days of her imprisonment. During the French Revolution she was imprisoned in the Carmelite monastery of Les Carmes—in the same cell, as a matter of interest, with Madame Tussaud, the originator of the wax-work exhibition near Baker Street. She later married the great Napoleon.

I do not think I can do better to describe her love for the breed than give two extracts, the first from Miss Estelle Ross's *Book of Noble Dogs,* and the second from *Josephine, Empress and Queen,* written by Frederic Masson in 1899:

> "Napoleon was not personally attached to dogs, though Josephine's little Fortune, who came into her possession when she was living at Carmes,[26] was used as a messenger between his mistress and Bonaparte, carrying little missives under his collar. He was no beauty, a bit of a mongrel, long in the body, low in the leg, russet-coloured, with the black muzzle and curly tail of a pug.
>
> "Josephine's fondness for Fortune nearly led to a quarrel with Napoleon on their wedding-night. Levy, in *La Vie Intime,* recalls a conversation which the general had with Arnault. Pointing to Josephine's dog lying on the sofa, he said:

" 'Do you see that gentleman: he is my rival. He was in possession of Madame's bed when I married her. I wished to remove him: it was quite useless to think of it. I was told that I must either sleep elsewhere or consent to share my bed. That annoyed me considerably, but I had to make up my mind. I gave way. The favourite was less accommodating. I bear proofs on my leg of what I say.'

"The general bore no grudge, for a few months later he wrote to his consort sending a 'million kisses even to Fortune, notwithstanding his naughtiness.'

"The favourite met a cruel fate in being killed by the cook's bull-dog,[27] and Napoleon hoped and intended that it would be the last of the Empress's favourites but she promptly provided a pug-dog as his successor—as she was exceptionally fond of this breed. The Emperor, in protest, interviewed the bull-dog assassin and suggested to him that he should devour the pug!

"The newcomer was very regular in his habits. As the lady of the bedchamber left the Empress for the night he followed her to her room—Napoleon had had his way as to another canine bedfellow—sleeping quietly on a chair by her bedside. In the morning, with his tail tightly curled, he waited in the ante-chamber till Josephine's door opened, which was his signal to rush in and overwhelm her with affectionate greeting."

Masson gives a long description of Josephine's dogs which, as will be seen from the following extract, were not always pug-dogs.

"The door is opened to admit the favourite dog, for none but Fortune had had the privilege of sleeping in his mistress's room and disputing the entree with Napoleon. Ugly as he was, however, short-legged, long-bodied, not so much tawny as red, with a nose like a weasel, and nothing but the face and the corkscrew tail to proclaim him a pug, Fortune had belonged to Josephine in

1793, and, when the Carmelite Monastery was her prison, the notes of warning or of safety were hidden underneath his collar. Fortune was gone; he had been strangled at Mombello by the cook's big dog. Josephine then adopted a female pet, and so much attached was she to the little animal that she sent for Moscati, the most celebrated physician in Milan, to attend it in an illness.

A painting by the famed German artist Wilhelm Busch.

This brought Moscati under Napoleon's notice and made his fortune. He became President of the Cisalpine Directory, deputy to the Council of Lyons, Director-General of Public Instruction, Count, Great Dignitary of the Iron Crown and senator of the kingdom, because he had not scorned such a patient. The little lap-dog's successor, a pug, had a place assigned to it in the carriage next after that of the Empress from the time of the Dieppe 'voyage' in the year XI. The pug was a personage well acquainted with etiquette, and never failed, when the dresser retired after the Empress was in bed, to follow her, whomsoever she might be, into her room, where he turned himself round on a chair, and there remained until morning. Then he would go down in a leisurely manner to the 'Salon d'annonce' and wait patiently until the door of his mistress's room was opened, when he would rush in with an air of wild delight and the liveliest demonstrations of affection. A brack-hound of the smallest species, given by M. de Colbert, failed, notwithstanding his hunting talents, to dethrone the pug, or rather the pugs, for there was a family of them. . . . These dogs had their own special 'bonne' (her name was La Brisee), and their keep in ordinary years varied from 350 to 450 fr., but in 1806 rose to 568 francs: they were with the Empress the whole day, lay close to her on the sofa, where she made a cushion for them of her 'cachemire,' announced visitors as well as the chamberlains and ushers, attacked everybody who approached their mistress, had a special liking for the red calves of Cardinals' legs, and would tear the robe that displeased them to rags, without any respect for its lining."

6
19th Century England

"A Pug did not suit me at all;
The feature unluckily rose up,
And folks took offence
When offering pence
Because of his turning his nose up."
G. T. Hood: "Lament of a Poor Blind"

E have now reached the great century in canine history. Many new breeds came into being and a much greater interest altogether was taken in the canine race.

So far as pugdom was concerned the greatest civil war that was ever known in dogdom was fought, concluding, rather like the Wars of the Roses, in the junction between the two houses of Morrison and Willoughby. Unfortunately, although the war was waged so recently, it is extremely difficult to give accurate dates. All the established facts were shattered by the Mayhew letter, and it seems certain that a mistake of, at least, a matter of twenty years has been made somewhere with respect to the Willoughby strain. But of this more anon.

The century opened badly so far as dogs were concerned. The whole country was agitated with internal industrial strife, and the threatened Napoleonic invasion kept everybody in a state of high nervous tension. People in those days did not realise that the famous Napoleonic star was a "dog star," and the divorce of Josephine and the separation from the influence of her pug-dogs was the moment from which Napoleon's fortunes waned, and Elba and St. Helena were to follow.

Not only was no breed of dogs popular at the beginning of the century, but it opened with a distinct and definite attack on the pug-dog.

The author of *The Sportsman's Cabinet,* published in 1804, threw down the gauntlet which, unfortunately, was not taken up till many years afterwards.

> "It is clear that the pug-dog, from its singularity, affords more doubt in the certainty of its origin than almost any of the species. It is asserted by some, that the genuine breed was introduced to this island from Muscovy, and that they were, originally, the undoubted natives of that country; others assert the pug to have been produced by a commixture between the English bull-dog and the little Dane, calling such races single mongrels, as coming from the mixture of two pure races; but there are other dogs which may, with propriety, be called double mongrels, because they come from a mixture of a pure race, and of one already mixed. The shock-dog, for instance, is a double mongrel, as being produced by the pug and the small Dane. The dog of Alicant is also a double mongrel, as coming from the whelp and small spaniel; and the Maltese, or lap-dog, is a double mongrel produced by the small spaniel with the barbet; the spaniel and the little dane produce the lion-dog,[28] which is very scarce....
>
> "For, perhaps, in the whole catalogue of the canine species, there is not one of less utility, or possessing less the powers of attraction than the pug-dog, applicable to no sport, appropriated to no useful purpose, susceptible of no predominant passion, and in no way whatever remarkable for any extra eminence, he is continued from era to era for what alone he might have been originally intended, the patient follower of a ruminating philoso-

An 1803 Pug, as pictured in *The Twentieth Century Dog,* **by Compton.**

pher, or the adulating and consolatory companion of an old maid."

This statement, upon which comment is superfluous, was not criticised till Hugh Dalziel, in 1888, said that the writer of the above quotation was

> "a cantankerous old bachelor, caring for nothing but his pipe, his pointer, and his gun ";

and Rawdon B. Lee, commenting on the quotation in 1894, writes:

> "The above is rather rough on the poor little pug, but such an unfair and ungallant description could only have emanated from the brain of a rough sportsman of the old school, whose chief delights would lay in badger drawing, bull baiting and cock fighting. The pug-dog has its uses in society, and possesses credentials as a lady's dog that cannot be excelled."

However, the description given in *The Sportsman's Cabinet* was accepted and did the breed great harm—much more, in fact, than the petty writers on canine matters who believed it to be amusing to vilify the breed during its popularity in the mid-Victorian era. One is glad, however, to be able to state that no writer on canine matters, whose works have been successful enough to be generally accepted and quoted at the present day, has criticised the pug-dog unfairly.

Early Willoughby Pugs, as portrayed in the 1881 edition of Stonehenge's *The Dogs of Great Britain, America and Other Countries.*

The writers on the subject, omitting writers on natural history, pure and simple, who have stood the test of time may be taken to be Idstone, G. R. Jesse, Stonehenge (J. W. Walsh), H. Dalziel, Rawdon B. Lee and, of a later day, W. D. Drury, Robert Leighton, James Watson and Edward C. Ash. Sometimes their criticisms may seem unkind, but they can be taken as none the less honest.

One rather amusing incident may be mentioned. Pug-dogs were given two new names at the beginning of the century, and these seem to have held to the breed for a considerable time: they were "the figure-of-eight dog" and "the jug-handled dog." The former name was, I take it, given to them because of their appearance either with regard to the tightly curled tail, or—which is even more likely—referring to the pug-dog's peculiar and characteristic walk when advancing towards any one, especially when he entertains pleasurable anticipations such as reciprocated affection, namely, a wriggling motion from side to side describing the semi-circular shape of the figure-of-eight; and the latter name has been explained by T. W. Knox in his *Dog Stories and Dog Lore,* published in 1887:

" 'Yes,' replied Mr. Graham, 'and this peculiar curve of the tail has given the pug the name of Jughandled Dog.'

" 'How is that?'

" 'Why, there's been a joke going the rounds of the papers that an enterprising dog-dealer had taken advantage of this peculiarity of the pug to make a handle by which he could be carried; by cutting a hole in the animal's skin, along his back, and grafting the tail into it until it became firm and the sore healed, it was asserted that a handle was formed by which the dog could be carried on a lady's arm like a workbag or hand-satchel, picked up to be transported over street crossings, or hung up on a nail or peg whenever desired.' There have been many absurd stories told about the pug, but this is the worst of all."

The reason for the great interest shown during the latter half of the nineteenth century in canine matters was due to a small spark struck at Newcastle-upon-Tyne in June 1859, when a gunmaker called Pape, whose shop is still extant in Collingwood Street of that city, offered a prize of some guns to the owner of the best pointer shown. Sixty dogs entered, and it was said that such a collection of dogs had never before been seen together. The excitement created by this show was immense, and dog shows were held in the same year at Birmingham and Edinburgh. Not only was England seized with the new sport of showing dogs, but even the Continent took up the game, and a show was held in Paris in 1865. Edward C. Ash, writing on the subject of these early shows, states:

"In the early show days of Birmingham (1860), the first show in which non-sporting dogs were catered for, was a class for pugs, but there appear to have been no entries. Leeds (1861) also had a class in which a first and second prize were awarded, but not the third. At the 1861 Manchester Show the prize-winner is given: '1st, the Female Blondin.' "

The popular enthusiasm for these shows led to the founding, by a Mr. S. E. Shirley, of a club for dogs in April 1873, so that shows might be regulated and the points of the various breeds defined.

The founding of this club, The Kennel Club, led to the formation of various clubs for special breeds, and The Pug Dog Club,[29] was early in the field. The first of the four British pug-dog clubs[30] which have been in existence, and which still retains its place at the present day, was founded in 1882, within ten years of the foundation of "The Kennel Club."

Ch. Loris, a top winner in the late 1800s, as pictured in the 1891 book, *Prize Pugs of America and England,* by Cryer.

The first Kennel Club Stud Book shows an entry of sixty-six pug-dogs, and amongst the pedigrees is given that of Cloudy, who will be mentioned hereafter:

> "Cloudy, 3756, bred by Lady Churston, by Mayhew's Click, out of Topsy; Click by Lamb (from Pekin) out of Moss."

Queen Victoria had a real love for dogs, but her chief affection was for her little dog Dash, a spaniel, and Waldman, a dachshund, whose grave is inscribed at Windsor: "The very favourite dachshund of Queen Victoria, who brought him from Baden, 1872; died, July 11, 1881."

Dash belonged to her mother, as the following extract from her diary, published by Viscount Esher, in 1912, under the title of *The Girlhood of Queen Victoria,* for the year 1833, will show:

> "*Tuesday, 15th January.*—I awoke at 7 and got up at 8. At 10 minutes to 9 we breakfasted. At half-past 9 came the Dean till half-past 1. Just before we went out, Mamma's little dog, a beautiful spaniel of King Charles's breed, called Dash, and which Sir John gave her yesterday, came and will now remain here."

She was so fond of this little dog that, after her coronation, C. P. R. Leslie tells us in his *Recollections* that:

> "When the state coach drove up to the steps of the palace, she heard the spaniel barking with joy in the hall, and exclaimed, 'There's Dash!' and was in a hurry to lay aside the sceptre and ball she carried in her hands, and take off the crown and robes *to go and wash little Dash.*"

But despite her love for Dash and Waldman and her other dogs, the Queen kept a fawn pug-dog in later years, but I cannot trace this dog's name; and she certainly had a terrible black creature with cropped ears and a white chest and feet, called a black pug-dog, in her kennels in 1854.

Pug-dogs were, as we have seen, extremely scarce at the beginning of the nineteenth century, and the earliest established breeder would appear to have been an innkeeper of Walham Green called Charles (or, more commonly, Charlie) Morrison, who bred the usual Dutch type of pug-dogs in a very small way about 1840. The Dutch type may be taken shortly to be, in comparison with present-day pug-dogs, light, clear, golden fawn,

An actual photo of Ch. Loris. From *Hutchinson's Dog Encyclopedia*

short nosed, with little wrinkle, massive in size, with a clearly defined, but thin, trace and thumb mark.

He was easily superseded by the more vigorous and pushful breeder, Mrs. Laura Mayhew, who commenced with the same type of dogs, but later introduced specimens imported from China. Other breeders of the day, in a minor way, were Mr. H. Gilbert and Mr. W. Macdonald, both of London. As Stonehenge says, the pug-dog

> "was exceedingly rare in the middle of the present" (nineteenth) "century, even a moderately good one not being procurable for less than £30, and that at a time when £5 was the average price of a lady's pet, even of the fashionable kinds."

Now, the efforts of Mrs. Mayhew excited Charlie Morrison to extend his breeding, and the introduction of Chinese blood into her strain gave his dogs a personality of their own which came to be known as "The Morrison Strain" or, more simply, "Morrison's." These efforts on the parts of the breeders started the pug-dog on his road to favour.

The Morrison strain is very important, so I will quote at length from Stonehenge, who was a friend of his:

> "According to Mr. Morrison's statement to me (which, however, he did not wish made public during his life), this strain was lineally descended from a stock possessed by Queen Charlotte, one of which is painted with great care in the well-known portrait of George III. at Hampton Court; but I could never get him to reveal the exact source from which it was obtained. That he himself fully believed in the truth of this story I am quite confident; and I am also of opinion that he never hazarded a statement of which he had the slightest doubt—being in this respect far above the average of 'doggy' men. Although he never broadly stated as much, I always inferred that the breed was obtained by 'back-stair influence,' and on that account a certain amount of reticence was neces-

sary; but, whatever may be the cause of the secrecy maintained, I fully believe the explanation given by Mr. Morrison of the origin of this breed of pugs, which is as commonly known by his name as that of Lady Willoughby de Eresby by hers. His appeal to the Hampton Court portrait, in proof of the purity of his breed from its general resemblance to the dog in that painting, goes for nothing in my mind, because you may breed up to any type by careful selection; but I do not hesitate to endorse his statement as to the Guelph origin of his strain, because I have full confidence in his truthfulness, from having tested it in various other ways. I need scarcely remark that both strains are derived from the Dutch—'the Morrison' coming down to us through the three Georges from William III., and 'the Willoughby' being a more recent importation direct from Holland and Vienna. Both strains are equally lively in temperament, moderately tricky and companionable, but their chief advantage as pets is that they are unusually free from smell both in breath and coat."

Now let us read what Stonehenge has to say with regard to the great rival of the Morrison strain, which afterwards got the name of the "Willoughby " strain.

"During the decade 1840-50, however, several admirers of pugs attempted to breed them from good foreign strains. Foremost among these was the then Lady Willoughby de Eresby, who after a great deal of trouble obtained a dog from Vienna which had belonged to a Hungarian countess, but was of a bad colour, being a mixture of the stone fawn now peculiar to the 'Willoughby strain,' and black; but the combination of these colours was to a certain extent in the brindled form. From accounts which are to be relied on, this dog was about twelve inches high, and of good shape, both in body and head, but with a face much longer than would now be approved of by pug-fanciers. In 1846 he was mated with a fawn bitch imported from Holland, of the desired colour, viz., stone fawn in body, with black mask and trace, but with no indication of

"...a terrible black creature with cropped ears and a white chest and feet..." is how the author describes Queen Victoria's black Pug, from 1854, shown here.

brindle. She had a shorter face and heavier jowl than the dog, and was altogether in accordance wlth the type now recognised as the correct 'Willoughby pug.' From this pair are descended all the strain named after Lady Willoughby de Eresby, which are marked in colour by their peculiar cold stone fawn, and the excess of black often showing itself, not in brindled stripes, but in entirely or nearly entirely black heads, and large 'saddle marks' or wide 'traces.' "

The points to be noted particularly in this statement by Stonehenge are the date at which Lady Willoughby commenced breeding and the origin of her strain. This is important, as it is the evidence of a contemporary writer, and other writers have followed him. So far as the Morrison strain is concerned I think we can accept Stonehenge, but I am going to suggest, for your consideration, that he was entirely wrong with regard to the Willoughby strain.

It will be noted that Stonehenge certainly makes no reference to the Mayhew strain, except stating that Mrs. Mayhew was an exhibitor "of late years," and if it would not be sacrilege to suggest it in connection with such an established authority, I cannot help suspecting that he has mixed up the early Mayhew strain with that of the Willoughby—though, again, I can trace nothing authoritative, except the statement of Stonehenge, with regard to the pug-dog imported from Vienna. However, Stonehenge's statement is important and must be given its full value.

Now let us consider the following letter from Reginald E. Mayhew of New York, son of Mrs. Laura Mayhew, which is published by James Watson in *The Dog Book:*

> "When shows were first promoted in England it was generally accepted that pugs had been imported to that country from Holland, Russia and China. How near or how wide of the mark were those responsible for this I will leave to others. I do know, however, that this was the opinion harboured by such authorities as Lord Willoughby D'Eresby, Charlie Morrison, Mr. Rawlins, Mr. Bishop and my mother.
>
> "At the outset the winning English pugs were of Dutch origin, and among the chief breeders were my mother and Mr. Morrison, the latter being landlord of an old-fashioned roadhouse, in the outskirts of Chelsea.
>
> "In those days pugs were cropped, and in general type were tight-skinned, straight-faced, apricot fawn in colour, and as a rule had good, wide-set eyes, which gave them a fairly good expression.
>
> "A few years afterwards—in the later 'sixties— Lord Willoughby became a prominent factor in pugdom, so much so that the term Willoughby pug was as common an expression in the breed as Laverack setter in English setters. Lord Willoughby, who lived near us at Twickenham, obtained his original specimens from a tight-rope walker known as the female Blondin, who brought them from St. Petersburg. They were silver fawns, the majority being smutty in colour, with pinched faces and small eyes, but better wrinkled than the Dutchmen.

"Reverting to their colour, I have seen so many born practically black in those old days, and consigned to the bucket on that account, that I have often marvelled that more recent exhibitors should have been so deluded as to consider the introduction of the black pugs a novelty. In fact, when Lady Brassey introduced the black variety her specimens had the inherent faults of the Willoughby strain—pinched faces, small eyes and legginess—plus tight skins. And so it is today, to a less marked degree, in specimens of this shading. In fact, the only really good-headed black I have seen here was Mrs. Howard Gould's Black Knight.

"With the advent of the smutty coloured Russians, breeders mingled their blood with that of the Hollanders, with the result that faces—through Rawlin's Crusoe, a good headed Dutchman—and Mr. Bishop's Pompey—bred half Dutch and half Russian—showed a slight improvement, while colour and shadings were a distinct advancement.

"Still, the winning specimens, typical as they were, lacked that grandeur in head which the ideal called for. Nor was it until my mother became the owner of Click that really grand heads and beautiful expressions were seen on the bench. Click has long been a household name in pugdom, as for more than twenty-five years the crack winners have traced back to him. In fact, all the great skulls, big, appealing eyes, square muzzles and short faces are due to Click. Chiefly through his daughter Cloudy—which was also owned by my mother—and in a minor degree through his union with Gipsey, a long-faced, undershot creature, belonging to Mrs. Lee, of Toy Spaniel fame, has his name become so closely associated with champions.

"Gipsey had three litters, containing specimens worthy of the highest praise. Unfortunately, however, Mrs. Lee, besides dogs, had in her cramped quarters a pet monkey, which, in spite of his owner's vigilance, succeeded in either killing the offspring or mutilating them. One of these was Odin, whose name is to be found in many pedigrees. In his case, the monkey had bitten off his tail to such effect that hardly any vestige of it was left.

"As to Click himself, he was an apricot fawn, with an ideal head and expression and most beautiful eyes. He was, on the leg, rather narrow behind, and as rough in coat as Mrs. Gould's Black Knight. In fact, alter the latter's colour and one would have a very good example of Click.

During the 1800s, Pugs were commonly featured on many advertising items. From the Flamholtz collection.

"Click's parents—Lamb and Moss—were Chinese beyond dispute. They were captured in the Emperor of China's palace during the siege of Pekin in 1867 or 1868, and were brought to England by the then Marquis of Wellesley, I think. Anyhow, they were given to a Mrs. St. John, who brought them several times to our house. Alike as two peas, they were solid apricot fawn, without a suspicion of white; had lovely heads and expressions; but, unlike their son, they were close to the ground, and a shade long in body. The pair were so much alike that my mother was firmly of the opinion they were brother and sister.

"I have purposely referred to the colour of Lamb and Moss, because when Click became a success as a sire, the story was circulated that his parents were lemon and white Japanese spaniels, and as few breeders had seen either Lamb or Moss the rumour was generally accepted.

"With the advent of Tragedy and his son Comedy,[31] the era of heads began. Both were colossal in stature, Tragedy being a dog in Scarborough so huge that he was called Tichborne, after the claimant. His (Tragedy's) dam, Judy, was by Click and from Mrs. Lee's Gipsey, while Comedy was by Tragedy from Cloudy, who, by the by, was an exceptionally good bitch, and should never have been beaten in the ring.

"I should say the best pugs I have seen are Miss Tacquet's Tum Tum, Mr. Booth's Comedy, Mrs. Foster's Jennie, Mrs. Britain's Little Count and Little Countess, Mrs. Maule's Little Duke, Miss Houldsworth's Dowager and Countess, and my mother's Hebe.

"I cannot leave the pug subject without expressing regret that popular feeling tends to hold the breed in a contemptuous cum ridiculous light. No breed in its specimens has such distinct individuality. In character the pug is brimful of intelligence; it is consequential to a degree; is willing to take its own part; does not possess an atom of shyness, and in the old days—when I was in swaddling clothes—and my parents lived in Derbyshire, the men used to take Tootie and her sons and daughters out ratting with ferrets. Being close and short-coated, pugs do not require half the attention called for by the more popular variety of toys, such as Pomeranians, Spaniels and Yorkshire terriers, while they are more robust in constitution and of a more independent spirit."

Commenting on this very interesting letter, James Watson writes:

"The information as to the Willoughby pugs is entirely new so far as we had any knowledge, and it rather dissipates the prevailing impression that certainly existed thirty years ago that the Willoughby pugs were an old and well-established strain. We recall the name of the female Blondin, but nothing as to the date she was performing in England. Blondin, after whom she was named, was there in 1858, so that if we say the Willoughby pugs date back to 1860, that will be near enough. This is borne out by what the stud book shows as to the introduction of the Willoughby blood into outside channels, for that appears to have first taken place about 1867, though one or two older dogs are said to have been of Lord Willoughby's strain. When it comes down to names, however, this seems to be the oldest pedigree we have: 'Mungo, born 1868, bred by Lord Willoughby, by his Ruby out of his Cora, out of his Mina. Ruby by Romeo out of Romah, out of Lady Shaftesbury's Cassy.' This is a peculiar pedigree, but even as it stands it is the exceptionally long one in the first volume of the stud book, which was anything but errorless as to names, breeding or reference numbers. The pedigree of Cloudy, the great brood bitch Mr. Mayhew refers to, is given as by Click out of Topsy, by Lamb out of Moss, whereas that is the Click extension.

"Mr. Morrison was as old a breeder as Mrs. Mayhew, probably older, and as his hostelry was a house of call for many persons, his pugs became well known. Outside of these West End of London breeders, there were many throughout England who owned, exhibited and bred pugs, but pedigree was very little thought of and very few pugs were equipped with one. We may take it, however, that the very great majority of the pugs, prior to the Willoughby and the Pekin introductions, were descendants of the Dutch pugs, or of pugs which came from China some time during the seventeenth century."

I would like to remind readers of the name of the winner of the Manchester Show of 1861, and to add that the Stud Book gives Click to be "by Lamb (from Pekin) out of Moss," and also mention that Leatherhead (George Lowe), in one of his *Pillars of the Stud-Book,* stated that Moss was said to be a Willoughby pug-dog.

This is all very confusing, I will admit, and it is one of my hopes that the publication of this book will bring forth information which will help the mystery to be cleared up as to how and when the Willoughby strain first started.

One is glad to be able to state, that however furious the fight was while it lasted between the adherents to the Willoughbys and the Morrisons, the battle was amicably settled by the interbreeding of the two strains, which proves that the League of Nations may do some good after all!

The Pug-Dog Club was founded, as we have seen, in 1882, by the efforts of Mr. T. Proctor; but it was not until 1887 that the points of the breed were settled, chiefly on those given by Stonehenge. The London and Provincial Pug Club was formed soon afterwards, and a separate standard of points, which were never adhered to, were drawn up by that society. Shows by the Pug-Dog Club are now held annually. There is a good description in *The Stock Keeper* of the 19th of June 1885 of the club show for that year, which proves that the club had held earlier shows and has probably held an annual show ever since its commencement:

" The Pug Club Show at the Aquarium has surpassed all similar undertakings in respect to gate-money. There is no mistake about pugs being first favourites with the fair sex. The gallery was full of ladies.

"Several of the winners wore necklaces. Miss Rennie's Lion (first prize) was bedecked

The early top winner Ch. George. From Cryer's Prize Pugs of America and England.

with a chaplet of turquoise beads, which were a source of much annoyance to the poor little chap, who kept catching his paws in the strings. This is exemplifying the French saying, 'Il faut souffrir pour etre beau.'

"The Pug Club had engaged the same show-man, whose vociferous efforts were equal to the occasion.

" 'Now then! Now then! Now then!!! This way for the Puggery. Come and see puggie, puggie, puggie!' "

It was by no means unusual for pug-dogs to wear valuable jewellery, and the pug-dogs belonging to the late Lord Anglesey were always bejewelled and expensively turned out.

Another reference to the breed in the same paper, *The Stock Keeper,* for April 1885, contains another peculiar announcement with regard to pug-dogs:

"PUG FRIGHTENED TO DEATH

"One of the entries at the Central Hall was that of the pug Lady Rosebud, but the bitch was absent, having died from frlght caused by being chased by another of her owner's pugs which was tied to a basket. The dog dragged this basket along, and so frightened Lady Rosebud and another, Prince Edward, that both died. The owner, Captain C. R. Harris, last year lost a pug under very similar circumstances. It was frightened to death by a tramp looking into the room through a window."

There can be no question that in the 'eighties the pug-dog was at the height of its popularity not only in this country but all over Europe; doubtless it nearly reached the height as that to which it will ascend in the present century. Hugh Dalziel, writing in 1888, states:

"As soon as the tide of fashion turned and again set in for pugs, the creation of the supply commenced, and now, like so many others, the Pug market is overstocked, and everywhere, in town and country, these animals swarm....Dogs of Pug character are widely distributed: a dog nearly akin to him is met with in China and Japan, he is well known in Russia, a favourite in Germany, plentiful in Holland and Belgium and common enough in France."

The chief publications of the nineteenth century on the most part were appreciative—J. C. Wood, in 1851, describing him as

"A cheerful and amusing companion, and very affectionate in disposition. Sometimes it is apt to be rather snappish to strangers, but this is a fault which is common to all lap-dogs which are not kept in proper order by their possessors. For those who cannot spend much time in the open-air it is a more suitable companion than any other dog, because it can bear the confinement of the house better than any other of the canine species; and, indeed, seems to be as much at home on a carpet as is a canary on the perch of its cage. Moreover, it is almost wholly free from the unpleasant odour with which the canine race is affected."

Idstone, in 1872, writes:

"I have seldom if ever seen a Pug-dog shy, snappish, or sulky; generally they are ready to be friendly with

During the heyday of the Pug, the breed was often featured on advertising items. These have become favored items for Pug collectors.

strangers—unexcitable and indifferent. Cleanliness is their chief attraction, and a certain high-bred demeanour....I cannot say that I am an admirer of their form...but their colour—exactly that of a mastiff—is, to my mind, exquisite."

And Rawdon B. Lee can be taken to sum up the evidence produced during the century when he wrote in 1894:

"As a companion in the house, and for an occasional run into the country, no dog is better fitted than the pug. He is cleanly in his habits, has a pretty, soft coat, and nice skin; no foul smell hangs about him, and he is gentleness itself. He shows no ill-temper or mopishness, and the objectionable lolling out of the tongue and unpleasant snorting, which at one time were so common in this variety, is quickly disappearing. Of several pugs that I have owned or known, not more than one of them was addicted to either of these unpleasant habits. All were lively and tractable, and if not actually as intelligent as a highly trained poodle, one pug I knew was quite accomplished in many little tricks he used to perform. No doubt had a professional trainer taken this little dog in hand, it would have been able to earn more than its own living on the stage. Again, a pug can remain sweet and healthy on less open-air exercise than any other dog, and two of them will play about the dining-room or nursery and amuse

These advertising cards were popular in the mid- to late 1800s.

Ch. Little Count was one of the standouts in 1887.

themselves as much as two terriers would by a scamper in the open fields.

"The pug is not a hunting dog, except as far as tracking the footsteps of his fair mistress is concerned, but he has been known to take to the unladylike occupation of killing rats, which he has done as well as a terrier. Still, it is no part of the duties of a lady's lap-dog to soil his pretty mouth by contact with the most obnoxious of creatures, because we all know that perhaps the next minute he may be fondled and caressed by his owner.

"Although I have said a pug-dog can do with comparatively little outdoor exercise, still, he is better for as much as he can be given, for no dog has a greater tendency to put on fat, and reach a state of obesity, than the one of which I write. Whoever saw a pug-dog thin and gaunt, with its ribs and backbone almost sticking through the skin? He always looks smooth, contented, and comfortable, eats well, and he should have as little meat and fat-producing food as possible. Some writers have given him the reputation of stupidity, but I do not believe him deserving of such an epithet. In the house and out of doors he is as sensible as any other dog, follows well in a crowd when properly trained, and is no more liable to lose himself than an ordinary terrier. Some friends of mine had what they called a pug, but she was not more than half or three-parts pure bred, who was particularly sensible. She would retrieve, kill rats, was fond of the gun, and liked a ride on the 'bus or tramcar so well that she continually would take one on her own account, which the kindly conductor allowed her to have gratuitously, the conditions of the 'tram' company notwithstanding. This dog had the curly tail, fawn colour, and general appearance of a pure-bred animal, excepting that she was rather long in face.

She lived to a great age, but as a rule the pug is not the longest lived of the canine race."

Towards the end of the century, however, the popularity of the pug-dog waned; the introduction of shows had brought new breeds into the arena, and novelty was the order of the day. Foremost among these new breeds, if one can call a dog a new breed which can carry its history back to 200 years B.C.—but a new breed from a popular point of view in this country—was the pomeranian. For some time the pug-dog kept up its prominence against the enormous numbers of pomeranians, which were being imported from Germany; but finally the advent of the pekinese drove it from its position of being the most popular toy-dog. The excitement created by the arrival of the pekinese was phenomenal, and no sooner had breeding started in earnest than all other breeds of toy-dogs were swept before it, and it attained the position it retains to this day of being the premier toy-dog.

Before ending this chapter I should like to mention a few of the outstanding pug-dogs of the nineteenth century. I have already mentioned the champions of the Mayhew, Morrison and Willoughby strains, but there are still a great many pug-dogs by other breeders who were famous during the late nineteenth and early twentieth century. I do not think I can do better than to give the list set out in *Cassell's New Book of the Dog:*

A litter sister to the dog on the previous page, Ch. Little Countess was a top winner in her own right. From Cryer's Prize Pugs of America and England.

"Mr. T. Proctor . . . has owned some very good dogs, of which Ch.

Confidence was one of the best. Confidence was a very high-class dog, correct in colour and markings, but was a size too big, as also was his son York, another remarkably fine Pug, correct in every other respect, and considered by many to be the most perfect fawn Pug of his day. He was exhibited by Mr. Proctor when a puppy, and

Ch. Stingo Sniffles topped many shows in the 1800s.

purchased at that time by Mrs. Gresham, who now also owns that charming little representative of his breed, Ch. Grindley King, who only weighs 14 lb., and is the perfection of a ladies' pet. Grindley King is one of the few Pugs that have a level mouth, and he is squarer in muzzle than most bigger dogs, whilst few Pugs have as much wrinkle and loose skin. He, however, has his faults, as he might be a little finer in coat, and he has not black toe-nails. The late Mr. W. L. Sheffield, of Birmingham, was an admirer of small Pugs, his Ch. Stingo Sniffles being a beautiful specimen and quite the right size. The late Mr. Maule's Royal Duke reminds one what a fawn Pug should be, and Mrs. Brittain had two famous Pugs, whilst Mr. Mayo's Ch. Earl of Presbury, Mr. Robert's Keely Shrimp, and Mr. Harvey Nixon's Ch. Royal Rip were very grand dogs. Mrs. Benson's Ch. Julius Caesar has had a successful career; he was bred by the late Mrs. Dunn, who owned a large kennel of good Pugs; and Miss Little's Ch. Betty of Pomfret was an excellent one of the right size. Another very beautiful little Pug is Mrs. James Currie's Ch. Sylvia."

To this list of the great ones may, I think, be added not unfairly two pug-dogs who helped to keep the breed in the limelight outside the show-ring—one on the stage, and the other in the courts.

The first is an extract from a newspaper of 1898:

> "This is an amazingly clever pug, belonging to Mr. and Mrs. B. Melville, who are well known in the entertainment world. This little dog takes the part of the 'coon' baby in a picturesque little stage spectacle. Dressed in baby's costume, she walks about the stage on her hind legs, looking very quaint, as you may imagine. After this sketch she goes through a performance entirely on her own account, merely looking to Mrs. Melville for the cue. This is one of the cleverest dog contortionists in the world. In the accompanying photo[32] we see that the animal has thrown herself into the favourite posture of human contortionists—a kind of reversed S. Mr. Melville will tell you that this little pug has a natural aptitude for performing, which renders a great amount of training quite superfluous."

The other pug-dog I have to mention caused a sensation in a law court, and the account is taken from the *Kennel Gazette* of January 1890:

> "Mr. Hannay recently had a case before him at Marlborough Street which puzzled him completely. Two ladies claimed a pug-dog as their own, and evidence was given by both sides in support of their respective cases. The dog made matters worse, for when one of the disputants called, 'Moppy, Moppy, come along, Moppy,' he evinced as much joy as if his owner was at last found. But when the other party to the suit called, 'Jem,' he went to her, and was equally obliging to any one who called. The magistrate found in this a loophole by which to escape the dilemma, to his evident relief, and he declined to make any order."

From *Modern Dogs*, by Rawdon Lee.

"(And then) I bought a dog—a queen!
Ah, Tiny, dear, departing pug!
She lives, but she is past sixteen,
And scarce can crawl across the rug.
I loved her, beautiful and kind;
Delighted in her pert Bow-wow;
But now she snaps if you don't mind;
'Twere lunacy to love her now.

I used to think, should e'er mishap
Betide my crumpled-visage Ti,
In shape of prowling thief, or trap,
Or coarse bull-terrier—I should die.
But, ah! disasters have their use;
And life might e'en be too sun-shiny:
Nor would I make myself a goose,
If some big dog should swallow Tiny!"

Calverley: Disasters

7

Black and Other Coloured Pugs

OU will recollect the statement by Mr. Reginald F. Mayhew, given in the last chapter, that he had seen many pug-dogs born practically black in the old days and confined to the bucket on that account, and, also, the dog belonging to Queen Victoria in 1854.

Rawdon B. Lee, discussing the question as to whether black pug-dogs were produced in this country before the introduction from China by Lady Brassey, writes:

> "Personally, I believe, there may be truth in both statements, that a black pug was accidentally produced and, at the same time, a specimen or two had been brought from the East."

But I have never heard of any pure black specimen being bred in this country prior to the Brassey introduction, though I have no doubt that had there been a demand for black specimens they could have been bred by carefully selective breeding of the darker fawn members, as there can be little doubt that many of the Russian and Chinese introductions had black ancestors.

There seems to be no doubt that Russia and, of course, China were breeding black specimens long before the blacks were known in this country.

W. D. Drury gives an account of the Brassey introduction. One of the dogs was called Mahdi, and Jack Spratt was the name of the other.

> "It was in the autumn of 1886 that black Pugs were first brought into notice, a class being given for them at the Maidstone Show, all the exhibits being from the kennel of the late Lady Brassey. Two or three of these were compact, good-coated specimens, Jack Spratt, whose name appears as sire of all the early specimens, being the largest that was benched. Where Lady Brassey obtained her first specimen was never then clearly stated; it was surmised that she became enamoured of a black Chinese Pug when she visited that country in the yacht the *Sunbeam,* and either purchased one, or mated a fawn female to a Chinese black dog. There is, however, some reason for thinking that black Pugs in England came from the fawns of King Duke's strain. Indeed, some breeders profess to have traced their history back to this dog. If they came from fawns, it seems just a little remarkable that they bred so true to colour as early as 1886."

I am given the date of the return of the *Sunbeam* to this country as 1884, and I have no doubt that this is approximately correct.

Frederick Gresham, writing in *Cassell's New Book of the Dog,* gives the names of the chief breeders and the best dogs after the introduction, to about 1909, but the present-day champions will be dealt with in the next chapter.

> "The black Pug is a more recent production. He was brought into notice in 1886, when Lady Brassey exhibited some at the Maidstone Show. Mr. Rawdon Lee,

however, tells us, in *Modern Dogs,* that the late Queen Victoria had one of the black variety in her possession half a century ago, and that a photograph of the dog is to be seen in one of the Royal albums. This, however, does not prove that a variety of black Pugs existed in any numbers....The black Pug, however, came upon the scene about the time mentioned, and he came to stay.

Lady Brassey, credited with importing black Pugs from China.

By whom he was manufactured is not a matter of much importance, as with the fawn Pug in existence there was not much difficulty in crossing it with the shortest-faced black dog of small size that could be found, and then back again to the fawn, and the thing was done. Fawn and black Pugs are continually being bred together, and, as a rule, if judgment is used in the selection of suitable crosses, the puppies are sound in colour, whether fawn or black. In every respect except markings the black Pug should be built on the same lines as the fawn, and be a cobby little dog with short back and well-developed hindquarters, wide in skull, with square and blunt muzzle and tightly curled tail. Her Majesty Queen Alexandra, when Princess of Wales, owned some very good black Pugs, but the first dog of the variety that could hold its own with the fawns was Ch. Duke Beira, a handsome fellow, who was the property of the late Miss C. F. A. Jenkinson. Then Mr. Summers startled the Pug world by buying the famous Ch. Chotee for £200. This price was, however, surpassed when the late Marquis of Anglesey gave £250 for Jack Valentine, who is still very much in evidence, sharing the hearthrug with his comrade Grindley King. Jack Valentine was bred by Miss J. W. Neish, who has a fine kennel of black Pugs at The Laws, in Forfarshire. Dr. Tulk has a famous stud dog in Ch. Bobbie Burns, who is probably the shortest-faced black Pug that has ever been bred; and a dog that has quickly forced his way to the front is Mrs. F. Howell's Ch. Mister Dandy, who is a beautiful specimen of the breed; but the biggest winner up to the present time has been Miss Daniel's Ch. Bouji, an excellent specimen all round, who has proved himself an exceedingly good stud dog. Amongst other prominent exhibitors and breeders of black Pugs are Mrs. Raleigh Grey—who, in Rhoda, owned one of the best females of the breed—Miss H. Cooper, Mrs. Recketts and Mrs. Kingdon."

There is a rumour that is continually cropping up amongst the ignorant and the malicious that the black pug-dog was created by a cross between the fawn pug-dog and a black pomeranian. There are certainly some grounds for this statement, and the cross has often been effected, particularly in France, but the result is not a black pug-dog. In England it would be called a Heinz hound

The black Pug, Ch. Impi, a winner at the turn of the century. From *British Dogs*, by Drury.

(forty different varieties), or a mongrel, but in France it has a name of its own—*Carlin a poil long.* These dogs resemble a black pug-dog, except that they have long silky coats and bushy tails which do not curl but are carried lightly over the back; and as they were, no doubt, known in England prior to the introduction of the black pug-dog, they gave some grounds for the assumption that the black pug-dog was produced somehow through the breeding of short-coated from the longcoated varieties. The late Queen Alexandra had a dog of this description, of whom she was very fond, called Quiz. Flatterers called it an Alicante, but there seems little doubt that it was a freak or a mongrel *Carlin a poil long.*

Rawdon B. Lee mentions a dog of this type:

> "Mrs. W. H. B. Warner, of Northallerton, at the close of 1893, showed a little black dog which she had brought from Japan, where it was said to be of a rare and choice breed. This is nothing else than a long-coated Pug—i.e pug in character and shape, but with a jacket such as is seen on a Pomeranian.

In opposition to this I find W. D. Drury mentioning long-coated pug-dogs which he, apparently, believed to have been formed without the pomeranian cross.

> "Rough-coated or long-haired Pugs are not very numerous, but they have appeared most frequently in the kennels owned by Mrs. Tulk and Miss Garniss. Only at intervals do they appear, and they always come from the strain owning Moss and Lamb as ancestors. These two dogs were said to have been 'captured' at Pekin well on to fifty years ago, and it is considered possible they may have had in their veins the blood of a long-coated Chinese dog. Mrs. Tulk has been successful in also breeding a long-coated black Pug."

In an interesting article upon pug-dogs, published in a paper on the 15th March 1902 under the signature of "La Vedette," the black pug-dog is described:

An S. T. Dadd drawing of a black Pug, which appeared in F. M. Archer's *The Dog in Health and Disease,* 1904.

"As a faithful, intelligent and sympathetic companion, a dog who can be merry and light of heart and feet, or quiet and gentle, according to your mood of the moment, no better recommendation could be made than that of the subject of these lines."

The same article, writing of the fawns in comparison with the blacks, continues:

"Besides being placid of temper they are usually excellent trenchermen, and perhaps a little given—for the pug is a dog quite clever enough to know wherein lie his strength and influence—to trading upon the supposed delicacy of lung and bronchial tubes which characterise the race, and thereby, by the apt and timely expedient of a hollow cough or a snuffle, avoiding the dull but necessary walk in the rain, and ensuring a continuance of the snooze by the fire.

"But in the case of the black brother all this is changed. There can be no doubt whatever that black and fawn pugs are of exactly the same race....At the same time, the black pug, unlike his human parallel, is a dog of far more lively and dominant personality than his pale brother. Black pugs have not that dislike to bad weather which occasionally confirms the fawns in evil courses, leading them to regard going out-of-doors in winter as more or less a penance; they are untiringly active dogs."

So far as I can trace, no white pug-dog has ever been produced, despite the statement by W. D. Drury that:

"White Pugs did not win any friends when a few of them were benched some years back.... We never see any exhibited now, or hear of them being bred."

I think we can take it that none had been seen up to the days of Idstone, 1872, who mentions that he had inquired of many breeders, but could hear of no white specimen ever having been known. Since the date of Idstone, however, two dogs described as "white" pug-dogs have been exhibited in New York, and Miss Dalziel exhibited one at Birmingham in 1892. Both Rawdon B. Lee and Frederick Gresham, however, state that none of these dogs were white but only very light cream-fawns.

The only other coloured pug-dog is Miss Bellamy's strain of blue pug-dogs, of which there is a beautifully stuffed specimen in the British Museum (Natural History section). This strain came to be formed in rather a peculiar way. Miss Little crossed a fawn bitch with a black dog, and in the litter were two cream puppies with chocolate markings, a pure chocolate, and, in another litter, a brown. A black son of this sire was the sire of the "Bellamy Blues." These blue pug-dogs are rare and have never been popular.

The future Queen Alexandra poses with her Pug and two Collies aboard the royal yacht, Osborne.

8

The 20th Century Pug

"The Pug (a diminutive and particularly ugly relative of the mastiff)."
J. R. AINSWORTH DAVIS, The Natural History of Animals, 1904.

I DO not intend to deal in this chapter with the respective merits of the various strains of pug-dogs exhibited at the present day, and I shall merely set out a schedule at the end of this book giving a list of the post-war champions and their owners. The best pre-war show dogs have been mentioned, and to go into the characters of the present-day specimens at any length would be out of keeping with the nature of this book, the intention of which is to give a short history of the breed during the 2600 years or so of its known existence. Further research by students into the earlier history of China will no doubt enable us to carry our history to an earlier date.

There can be no doubt that the pug-dog is increasing in numbers and popularity all over this country, and I trust that it will not be long before it regains the place to which it has always been entitled at the head of the list of toy-dogs.

To deal, however, with the history of the pug-dog in this century. At the beginning of the twentieth century the pug-dog was not popular. The pekinese was easily first favourite, and was followed by the pomeranian and toy-spaniels running fairly close together. The pug-dog took a rather poor fourth place.

The breed was subject to the usual attacks on the fallen from high estate, and it suffered from being a victim of the ancient and dishonourable sport of "kicking a dog when it's down."

Edwin Noble in his *Dog Lover's Book,* published in 1910, proved himself no pug-dog lover. The following are extracts from his book:

Ch. Bouji, owned by Miss. F. M. Daniels. From The New Book of the Dog, by Leighton.

"Occasionally one sees a motor-car dashing through the London streets, and inside, seated beside the owner, will be a little dog wearing a pair of motor goggles, a little motor coat, a bell hanging from his blue collar, of course, and in wet, cold weather even a pair of warm gloves or shoes upon his forefeet. You cannot see very much of the dog himself, but you have no need to look twice to see that it is a Pug-dog—for no other dog would submit to being made such a 'Guy.' . . .

"The best stories which stand to the Pug's credit are one in which, after an absence of two and a half years, he recognises the maid who used to wash him, and another in which a Pug-dog used to carry a collecting-box upon his back to collect funds to provide luxuries for our troops during the South African War; when he met anybody he would deliberately stop and shake his box to attract their attention."

But Mr. Noble hastens to add, and at length, that any other breed could have done the same things, only very much better!

I take the first extract from Mr. Noble's book to be a compliment in showing the placidity of the pug-dog in submitting to the wishes of his owners even if they are unpleasant. But, as a matter of fact, I believe Mr. Noble has mistaken the breed, as I have never heard of a pug-dog "guyed" in the fashion he mentions, though the French bulldog certainly suffered from this form of imbecility in its owners. I do not deny that pug-dogs at the beginning of this century often had bells on their collars like other toys.

But there were other writers willing to give the pug-dog his due, and C. H. Lane, in his *All about Dogs,* published in 1900, describes him as follows:

> "One of the really old-fashioned pets and companions is the Pug, of which I have for the last thirty years generally had some specimen in my house, and usually, when I have judged the breed, have been favoured with record entries. I remember on one occasion, when I had a very heavy day at an important London show, and had taken an immense amount of trouble, in the open, on a broiling day in June or July, when the whole of my exhibitors were of the fair sex, and ranged from the highest in the Kennel-world, Her Royal Highness, the Princess of Wales, to those who would not be ashamed to be included amongst 'the working classes.'
>
> "A very smart, showy and active dog, often *an arrant coward,* but with a great appearance of dignity, and even ferocity, which is not without its impression on the public. My experience of the breed is that they are, as a rule, very affectionate, and devoted to their owners,

York is typical of Pugs shown in the early 20th century. He was owned by Mrs. Gresham.

'gooddoers' and nearly always ready for anything in the way of eating and drinking, great lovers of comfort, and very jealous of any other members of the doggy community being made as much of as themselves. They are very lively, bustling companions, and very popular with those who have kept them."

F. T. Barton, too, wrote at length on the pug-dog in his *Our Dogs and All About Them,* from which I have extracted the following:

"This is a very old variety of Toy-dog, and one that always maintains its popularity, though, to a considerable extent, it has been displaced by such breeds as the Pomeranian, the Pekinese, etc., etc.; yet, in spite of this, as a dog for companionship for children, it has certainly no superior, even if it has any equal.

"Successive generations of such associateship have conferred upon it that degree of docility so essential for such purposes.

"No amount of provocation seems to disturb the temperament of the Pug, yet, in spite of this, it can be obstinate to a degree, such obstinacy usually revealing itself during the forcible administration of medicine, etc., etc....

"The Pug was introduced into Great Britain from China....

"At one time attempts were made to breed white Pugs, but the experiments were not carried far enough. . . . As a breed the Pug is hardy."

A top winner in the early 1900s, Ch. Grindley King, owned by Mrs. Gresham.

The forbearance of the pug-dog with children, which Mr. Barton mentions,

Ch. Master Jasper poses with his many medals. He was owned by Miss L. Burnett and is pictured in Leighton's *The New Book of the Dog*.

was very early recognised, and there is rather a gruesome description of a case of this in Lieut.-Col. Charles Hamilton Smith's *Mammalia,* in "The Naturalist's Library," which was published in 1840:

"We have witnessed forbearance in one" (pug-dog) "belonging to a lady, whose child bit the dog until he yelled, but never showed anger, or a disposition to get away."

I would like just to mention the names of two people who have been great pug-dog lovers during this century, and both of whom have passed away. Both bred and kept pug-dogs, and both did the breed the greatest possible good in their different stations of life. The first is the late Queen Alexandra and the second is my old friend, the late Mr. Courtney Thorpe.

I can only find one trace of the breed being kept by the present Royal family. This was in an article appearing in *The Ludgate,* for October 1897. In this article it is stated that the then Duchess of York (now H.M. the Queen) had a burial-ground for her pet dogs at Oaklands Park in Surrey. The article is illustrated by a photograph of various canine tombstones, on one of which I can decipher the following words: "Topsy a pug and Dinah her . . . mother."

Having dealt with some owners I will mention one pug-dog. The following extract is taken from a cutting from *Lloyd's Newspaper* in 1905:

"A pug that lives in Richmond has been taught to let the cat climb on his back and to carry her round the room to dinner. They both dine off the same plate. When the meal is finished the mistress says to the Pug, 'Now,

Sam, make Toushan pay for her dinner.' Sam then growls, and strikes puss on the face with his paw, a familiarity which the cat resents by boxing the dog's ears."

In the north of England, and in Scotland in particular, an increase in the popularity of the breed has been shown during the past few years, and it was found necessary for a new club to be created. This was The Scottish Pug-Dog Club, of which the first president was Miss Hatrick and the first hon. secretary was Miss M'Kay. The club was founded in 1925. The present president and hon. secretary are, respectively, Mr. R. E. M'Nair and Mrs. M'Craw of 38 West Bowling Green Street, Leith.

Pug-dogs of this country are now being bred slightly smaller than their Victorian brothers, and the breed is living up to the title it was given long ago of being "the grand little breed," and it is fulfilling the motto given it by the Pug-Dog Club of "Multum in parvo."

I am very glad to be able to say that all over the country the sterling worth of the "grand little breed" is being realised. The fact of its great gift of perfect health and the very little trouble needed to keep it always in perfect condition, is at last being accepted, and gives it a great pull over the long-coated breeds of toy dogs. I would like to end with that one particular quality which has been noted from the very earliest days. In the words of W. D. Drury:

> "One quality they possess above most breeds, which is a strong recommendation for them as lap-dog, and that is their cleanliness, and freedom from any offensive smell of breath or skin."

9
The Pug in America

"After the close of the Napoleonic Wars he" (the pug-dog),
"found his way across the Channel to England...."
Captain A. H. Trapman: *The Dog: Man's Best*
Friend. 1929.[33]

HE fashions in dogs in the United States of America seem to fluctuate in very much the same way as they do in this country, but to a less marked extent, though the favourite breed appears always to be the same in the two countries.

The popularity of the pug-dog here in about 1880 was echoed slightly later in the U.S.A., by a large increase in its pug-dog population. And, again, the advent of the pekinese here was felt in the U.S.A. towards the beginning of this century. Today, both in the U.S.A. and here, by far the most popular toy-dog is the pekinese.

Before the European discovery of America, three breeds of dog are said to have been known in South America. "The largest of these was an animal of medium size, with slender head and legs.... The second was a short-legged dog, somewhat resembling a dachshund, which, to judge from a vase-painting, was also used in the class. The third was a kind of pug, probably kept as a lap-dog."[34] But apart from these natives it seems difficult to trace the arrival of the first Christopher Columbus pug-dog. Specimens, no doubt, crossed over with the settlers in the early eighteenth century during the time of the popularity of the breed in this country. They were clearly known at the time of Washington Irving (1783-1859).

When dog-shows began in the U.S.A., the breed was taken up by Dr. Cryer, and the history of American pugdom may be said to have really started with this gentleman.

Dr. Cryer was the author of a book written exclusively on pug-dogs, and he did a tremendous amount of good for pug-dog breeding in the U.S.A. Nearly all the early show specimens were imported from this country, and, as we will see, were nearly all of the Mayhew strain.

I do not think I can do better than to quote at length from James Watson, who wrote from the U.S.A., and gives the American point of view:

> "The usefulness of the Click blood seems to have been in the production of successful dams, for outside of Odin and Toby, the sire of Dr. Cryer's Dolly, it is hardly possible to trace back to Click in the male line. On the other hand we find, in that very hard-to-get and useful book Dr. Cryer published in 1891, *Prize Pugs,* his extensions of pedigrees of the leading winning dogs of America up to that time show that fifty per cent of them, and those including nearly all the best dogs, had this Click cross. Bob Ivy, Dr. Cryer's best production, had three crosses, being inbred to Dolly on the sire's side, and Dolly was by Toby, and on the dam's side going back to Vic, by Click out of Leech's or Lock's Judy. This Vic was also the dam of Tum Tum II., a remarkably good dog by Max. Imported Othello also traces to Vic. From the Click-Gipsey cross we find Judy, dam to Tragedy, and from the Click-Topsy came Cloudy, who was dam of Comedy, also of Dowager the dam of Queen Rose and Duchess of Connaught. Queen Rose was dam of Champion Loris. Cloudy was also dam of Lady Flora, whose daughter, Lady Cloudy, was the dam

P. Frenzeny's drawing of Ch. George, winner of Best Pug at the seventh Westminster Kennel Club Show, as shown in Harper's Weekly, in 1883. From the Flamholtz collection.

of Kash, a prominent winner here in 1889 and 1890.

"There was quite a run on the get of the dog Toby on the part of American exhibitors after Dr. Cryer's Dolly had made her mark, and Lord Nelson and Miss Whitney's Young Toby were by him. Toby was by Click out of Mrs. Mayhew's Hebe, by Crusoe out of Phyllis, a part Willoughby bitch. Notwithstanding we had some close-up descendants of this inbred Pekin strain of pug, not one of the entire number that were exhibited showed any indication of the build of Lamb and Moss, the long and low type which Mr. Mayhew says they were, and which we see in most of the long-haired Pekinese which have come direct from China to England or here. Dr. Ivy, father of the then little boy after whom Dr. Cryer named his best production, very kindly sent us from Shanghai photographs of what the owner named Pekin Pugs, and Dr. Ivy said the dog was a high-class specimen. This we submitted to Mr. Mayhew to see how the dog might conform to his recollection of Lamb and Moss, and he replied as follows: 'There is no more resemblance to Lamb or Moss than to any pug of the present day. Neither Lamb, Moss nor Click had a white hair, nor had any of the latter's progeny. The dog is apparently a smooth Pekinese, just as there are smooth-coated specimens in the rough-coated varieties of terriers. Lamb, Moss and Click were as profuse coated as are the descendants of a certain line of smooth fox terriers. A very large proportion of Click's sons and daughters, however, had the orthodox length of coat, nor was it transmitted in subsequent generations.'

"The first pug of quality shown in this country was Dr. Cryer's Roderick, a dog of nice size, handicapped by very straight hind legs to the extent of being double jointed. It was this defect that enabled Mrs. Pue's larger dog George to defeat him in the majority of cases when they met. Both of these dogs were inferior to little Banjo, which was one of the kennel of dogs brought over in 1881 by Mr. Mason, but which unfortunately was smothered while in transit to London, Ont., show that fall. He was the sire of Lovat, one of the very best show dogs and sires of his day in England. Of the bitches of that time the best by a good margin was Mr. Knight's Effie, which won in

Eberhardt Kennels advertised their stud, Ch. Loki, in 1902.

the open class at New York in 1882, beating Dr. Cryer's Dolly. Effie afterwards won three championships at New York, but unfortunately she was a non-breeder. The next good pug was the dog which was here known as Joe, but whose proper name was Zulu II., the change of name being the result of an error on the part of the young man sent over from England in charge of Miss Lee's dogs. The real Joe was sold as Zulu II. before the dogs went to Pittsburgh show, and Zulu II. was shown as Joe and got second to Sambo. Dr. Cryer wanted to buy 'Joe' and offered the catalogue price of fifteen pounds to the secretary of the show, who declined it, saying that he had bought the dog. The fact is that the young man had found out his mistake and got the officials to protect him. Coming back to New York the young man got short of funds, and left the dog to pay his board bill; the owner then went to Mr. Mortimer, who recognised the dog and bought him, and at the New York show of a few weeks later, Joe appeared in his new owner's name, and won. There was quite a little talk about the seeming peculiarity of these proceedings, but it was all cleared up and the *bona fides* of Mr. Mortimer's purchase thoroughly established. Joe, as he continued to be called, was by Comedy out of a pedigreeless bitch, and he continued his successful career till 1887, winning altogether twelve championships, most of them for Mr. George H. Hill, of Madeira, O. He was also the sire of a number of good pugs.

"After Joe the next good dog imported was Bradford Ruby, a son of Lovat. An excellent pug, just a trifle large, and slightly leggy. This dog had won many prizes before being imported, but when he made his first appearance here at the New York show, the late Hugh Dalziel, who ought to have not only known what a good pug was, but also known what this pug was, gave Bradford Ruby a v.h.r. card. There were sixteen dogs in the open class, which shows how popular pugs were at that time, but all the good dogs were in the v.h.r. division, and the three placed animals were plain, ordinary specimens, not

Ch. Bradford Ruby was a top winner for several years in American shows.

one of which distinguished himself after that. As it was now necessary to win three firsts in open class, Bradford Ruby's record in the latter class is not so good as that of Joe, but he won nine firsts in the champion class. After Ruby came Master Tragedy, Othello and Lord Clover, none of them in the class of Ruby. Othello was really the best of the three, but he was rather large and his colour smutty. Master Tragedy fell far short of what we expected on his English reputation.

"The home-bred pugs of Dr. Cryer now became the prominent feature in the breed, beginning with his Max and Bessie, both out of imported Dolly, who was by the Click dog Toby. Then came Dude, also out of Dolly, but he was sold, and finally Dude's son Bob Ivy. 'Little Bob' was a fitting culmination to the doctor's breeding, for business now compelled him to gradually give up the fascinations of improving and showing pugs. Bob Ivy was a very nice little dog in every way, and his size was all one could desire. Bessie used to beat him for the specials for best in the show, but after the little dog had matured he was hard to beat. In front of him at New York in 1890 was a very smart young imported dog, Tim, by the English dog Max, but he died the same year.

"As the pedigree of Bob Ivy covers the ground very fully for most of the pedigree of dogs of that time, we give it in full:

"Bob Ivy"

Bred and owned by Dr. M. H. Cryer; born April 23, 1888

Pedigree.

```
                                  ┌ Ch. Punch (E. 6761)
                    ┌ Ch. Roderick┤ By Lord Willoughby's
         ┌ Ch. Max  │              └ Jumbo.
         │          └ Imp. Dolly . Morris' Judy.
Sire:    │                     ┌ Click ┌ Lamb, from Pekin.
Ch.      │              ┌ Toby │       └ Moss, from Pekin.
Dude     │              │      │ Hebe  ┌ Crusoe.
         │              │             └ Phyllis ┌ Tomahawk.
         │              │                       └ Fatima II. ┌ Jumbo.
         └ Imp. Dolly   │                                    └ Fatima.
                        │       ┌ Ch. Punch
                        └ Liz.  └ Molly, by Ch. Baron ┌ Cupid.
                                                      └ Ruby.

                                   ┌ Skylark    ┌ Guss.
                        ┌ Othello  │            └ Eden.
         ┌ Imp. Othello │          └ Judy
         │              │          ┌ Tum Tum II.. Max ┌ Sam.
Dam:     │              └ Scamp II.│                  └ Rose.
Vesta    │                         │                    ┌ Click ┌ Lamb.
         │                         └ Belle Petite . Vic │       └ Moss.
         │                                              │ Leech's
         └ Imp. (Pedigree unknown).                     └ Judy.
```

"Pugs went on the down grade after 1890, and with the arrival of new attractions in the way of toy-dogs, such as Pomeranians, and the pushing of Japanese and English spaniels to the front, they became fewer by degrees and beautifully less, until we have now to rely almost entirely upon one exhibitor, the well-known Al. Eberhardt, of Camp Dennison, O. It looked at one time as if there might be a turn for the better, that being when Mrs. Howard Gould was showing a few black pugs, but they did not catch on as they should have, and it is Eberhardt's pugs or a blank at nearly all the shows for the past year or two.

"There is no reason why this breed should be neglected in this way. Compare the pug with any of the popular fancies and it will stand the test. Tastes differ, but to our mind the character and beauty of wrinkle in the head of such a dog as Ding Dong is far ahead of the abnormally developed Japanese spaniel, for instance. Look at the care called for by these longcoated dogs, and the impossibility of making a pet and companion of any of the long, silky-coated toys. The pug needs no more coddling than a hardy terrier, nor any more care in

The bitch, Ch. Bo-Peep, was an early winner at Midwestern shows.

coat. He is a dog that has always had a reputation for keeping himself clean and tidy, and they used to say that he had less doggy perfume than any other house dog. He may not be quite so demonstrative as some of the effervescing little toys, but he is just as intelligent and has a dignity and composure all his own.

"Ere long we fully expect to see the black pugs become popular, for they are certainly very attractive in their brilliant coat of black satin. As Mr. Mayhew says, they are apt to be 'tight-skinned' and fail to show the wrinkle such as Ding Dong displays; but a few do show improvement in that direction, and it is only a matter of careful selection and breeding such as one has to carry out in all breeds to reach success. There is a good field here for those who want to take up something that is bound eventually to become a popular breed."

From the day of which Mr. Watson writes to the present, there has not been a revival of the breed in the U.S.A., and the beauties of the black have not been appreciated there. This is a joy for them which is yet to come. Registrations at the American Kennel Club were fifteen in 1926 and only three for the months January to November inclusive during 1927, against the 283 registered in England in 1927. But it is interesting to note that for the year 1926, apart from the pekinese which scored 229 registrations against 3627 in England (1927), and the pomeranian which scored 96 against our 1412 (1927), the pug-dog secured more registrations than any other toy-dog in the U.S.A.

The demand from the U.S.A. for the exportation of good pug-dogs from this country has, however, of recent years, been slowly but surely increasing. Mrs. Power, of Birmingham, has sent across some good dogs during the last few years.

I, too, have sent recently two fawn bitch puppies to purchasers in Canada, and it has been my experience, which I have no doubt other breeders will endorse, that, with regard to pug-dogs, once planted in a new country or district they quickly bear fruit. He is seen, hardly believed and an immediate demand comes for further specimens.

10
Show Points

HAVE set out below the standard of show points drawn up by Stonehenge and published in his *Dogs of the British Islands,* in 1878, which preceded by over five years the first list of show points issued by the Pug-Dog Club. Below it I have given the latest standard of points issued by the Pug-Dog Club.

A few words, however, are necessary before the Stonehenge points can be clearly understood.

It was a common practice of breeders of bull-dogs to cross their dogs with pug-dogs, and most of the winning bull-dogs in the early show days had the pug-dog cross. This was naturally opposed by the breeders of pug-dogs, and pug-dogs with a trace of the bull-dog in them were regarded with the greatest disfavour.

This practice started in very early days, George Edwards (1694-1773) mentioning in his chapter on "Bull-dogs" that "Dutch mastiffs or pug-dogs" were used "by accident or design" to "improve the bulldogs." Stonehenge also mentions the practice in his day, and Frederick Gresham, in *Cassell's New Book of the Dog,* writes that:

"It is known that it" (the pug-dog) "has been bred with the Bull-dog for the anticipated benefit of the latter."

It is with this in mind that we must consider the standard issued in 1878 by Stonehenge.

POINTS OF THE MODERN PUG

	Value.		Value.		Value.
Head	10	Trace	5	Legs and feet	10
Ears	5	Colour	10	Tail	10
Eyes	5	Coat	10	Symmetry and size	5
Moles	5	Neck	5		
Mask, vent and wrinkles	10	Body	10		
	35		40		25

GRAND TOTAL . 100

1. The *head* (value 10) should have a round, monkey-like skull, and should be of considerable girth, but in proportion not so great as that of the bull-dog. The face is short, but, again, not "bully" or retreating, the end being cut off square; and the teeth must be level—if undershot, a cross of the bull is almost always to be relied on. Tongue large, and often hanging out of the mouth; but this point is not to be accepted for or against the individual. The cheek is very full and muscular.

2. The *ears* (value 5) are small, vine-shaped and thin, and should lie moderately flat on the face (formerly they were invariably closely cropped, but this practice is now quite out of fashion); they are black, with a slight mixture of fawn hair.

3. The *eyes* (value 5) are dark brown and full, with a soft expression. There should be no tendency to weep, as in the toy spaniel.

4. A *black mole* (value 5) is always demanded on each cheek, with two or three hairs springing from it; the regulation number of these is three, but of course it is easy to reduce them to that number.

5. *Mask, vent and wrinkles* (value 10). These markings must be taken together, as they all depend mainly on colour. The wrinkles, it is true, are partly in the skin; but over and above

these there should be lines of black, corresponding with them, on the face and forehead. The mask should extend over the whole face as jet black, reaching a little above the eyes, and the vent should be of the same colour. In the Willoughby strain the black generally extends higher up the skull, and has not the same definite edge as in the Morrison pug, in which this point is well shown and greatly insisted on by its admirers.

6. A *trace* (value 5) or black line is exhibited along the top of the back by all perfect pugs; and the clearer this is, the better. As with the mask, so with this—the definition is more clear in the Morrison than in the Willoughby pug. When it extends widely over the back it is called a "saddle mark," and this is often displayed in the Willoughby, though seldom met with in the Morrison strain; of course, it is admired in the one, and deprecated in the other, by their several supporters.

7. The *colour* (value 10) of the Morrison pug is a rich yellow-fawn, while that of the Willoughby is a cold stone. The salmon-fawn is never met with in good specimens of either, and is objected to. In the Willoughby the fawn-coloured hairs are apt to be tipped with black, but in its rival the fawn colour is pure, and unmixed with any darker shade. Of course, in inbred specimens the colour is often intermediate.

8. The *coat* (value 10) is short, soft and glossy over the whole body, but on the tail it is longer and rougher. A fine tail indicates a bull cross.

9. The *neck* (value 5) is full, stout and muscular, but without any tendency to dewlap; which again indicates, when present, that the bull-dog cross has been resorted to.

10. The *body* (value 10) is very thick and strong, with a wide chest and round ribs; the loin should be very muscular, as well as the quarters, giving a general punchy look, almost peculiar to this dog

11. *Legs and feet* (value 10). The legs should be straight but fine in bone, and should be well clothed with muscle. As to the feet, they must be small, and in any case narrow. In both strains the toes are well split up; but in the Willoughby the shape of the foot is catlike, while the Morrison strain has a hare foot. There should be no white on the toes, and the nails should be dark.

12. The *tail* (value 10) must curve so that it lies flat on the side, not rising above the back to such an extent as to show daylight through it. The curl should extend to a little more than one circle.

13. *Size and symmetry* (value 5). In size the pug should be from 10 to 12 inches high—the smaller the better. A good specimen should be very symmetrical.

I present the points now in force and drawn up by the Pug-Dog Club, without comment:

Symmetry.—Symmetry and general appearance, decidedly square and cobby. A lean, leggy Pug and a dog with short legs and a long body are equally objectionable.

Size and Condition.—The Pug should be *multum in parvo*,

REVISED STANDARD OF POINTS OF THE PUG-DOG CLUB

	Fawn. Points.	Black. Points.
Symmetry	10	10
Size	5	10
Condition	5	5
Body	10	10
Legs / Feet	5	5
Head	5	5
Muzzle	10	10
Ears	5	5
Eyes	10	10
Mask	5	—
Wrinkles	5	5
Tail	10	10
Trace	5	—
Coat	5	5
Colour	5	10

but this condensation (if the word may be used) should be shown by compactness of form, well-knit proportions, and hardness of developed muscle. Weight, from 14 to 18 lb. (dog or bitch) desirable.

Body.—Short and cobby, wide in chest and well ribbed up.

Legs.—Very strong, straight, of moderate length, and well under.

Feet.—Neither so long as the foot of the hare, nor so round as that of the cat; well-split-up toes, and the nails black.

Muzzle.—Short, blunt, square, but not upfaced.

Head.—Large, massive, round—not apple-headed, with no indentation of the skull.

Eyes.—Dark in colour, very large, bold and prominent, globular in shape, soft and solicitous in expression, very lustrous, and, when excited, full of fire.

Ear.—Thin, small, soft, like black velvet. There are two kinds—the "Rose" and "Button." Preference is given to the latter.

Markings.—Clearly defined. The muzzle or mask, ears, moles on cheeks, thumb-mark or diamond on forehead, black-trace should be as black as possible.

Mask.—The mask should be black. The more intense and well-defined, the better.

Wrinkles.—Large and deep.

Trace.—A black line extending from the occiput to the tail.

Tail.—Curled tightly as possible over the hip. The double curl is perfection.

Coat.—Fine, smooth, soft, short and glossy, neither hard nor woolly.

Colour.—Silver or apricot-fawn. Each should be decided, to make the contrast complete between the colour and the trace and the mask.

There is no need to set out in full the show points issued by the Scottish Pug-Dog Club in 1925, as they are very similar to those of the Pug-Dog Club.

The "acknowledged points" are almost word for word the same, with the exception of the weight, which is given by the Scottish Club as "from 13 to 17 lb. (Dog or Bitch)."

The "standard of points" varies very slightly. Both blacks and fawns are given 10 points for legs and feet, whilst the tail is only given 5.

11
Footnotes

1. This book was chiefly written in 1928, and the registration figures, except when otherwise stated, are based upon the Kennel Club returns for 1927, and the American Kennel Club returns for 1926.

2. *A Guide to the Domesticated Animals exhibited in the Central and North Walls of the British Museum (Natural History),* 1908.

3. In spite of the short face produced by modern breeders, which is the first point generally looked for and admired in a good pug-dog, it is interesting to note that present-day judges usually insist on even sets of teeth. A crowded mouth of teeth, or such teeth as are described above, should handicap any pug-dog in the show-ring. There is no reason why a pug-dog's teeth should not be as even as the best terrier's mouthful. Pug-dogs' teeth are usually stronger and bigger than those of other toy breeds, such as the pekinese *(sic)* and the pomeranian. Presumably animal denistry was not so advanced in those days. It is usual, nowadays, to remove any milk teeth from a pup's mouth, should it have too many, which can easily be done by a qualified veterinary surgeon. How-

ever, I have seen modern pug-dogs with the shortest possible faces and perfectly even sets of teeth. These particular dogs' teeth had grown quite naturally and they had had none removed. Of course, it must be taken into consideration that we know more about feeding all dogs, and have better foods for them, than did our ancestors. All this plays a great part in the health of a dog's teeth. Even twenty years ago, when the above extract was written, doubtless the erroneous method of feeding pet-dogs on slops was still prevalent.

4. *A History and Description of Modern Dogs,* 1894.

5. *Cassell's New Book of the Dog,* edited by Robert Leighton.

6. *E.g.* "The Naturalist's Library," *Mammalia,* Lieut.-Col. Chas. Hamilton Smith, 1840.

7. I am referring, of course, to the Chinese mastiff.

8. "The dog was certainly found on the General Post Office site..." From *A letter from the British Museum.*

9. This word used to be the name for "Russia" in Chinese.

10. *Dogs: Their History and Development.*

11. Any type of small, short-legged and small-headed dog.

12. The Palace dog was rigorously conserved to one uniform unicoloured type of sleeve dog, always having a dark red coat and black mask.

13. V. W. F. Collier, *Dogs of China and Japan.*

14. The nickname approximately means "Pug-dog Sung."

15. 1572

16. "For, as a spaynel, she wol on hym lepe" (Chaucer, 1386). "A good spaynel shulde not be rough, but his taile shulde be rough." (*Master of the Game,* 1410).

17. *Dogs of China and Japan*

18. "His colour was isabel, a name given in allusion to the whimsical vow of Isabella Clara Eugenia, Governess of the Netherlands, at the memorable siege of Ostend, which lasted from 1601 till 1604." (Dillon: *Travels in Spain,* 1781)

19. "Howbeit one thing is not here to be omitted, as a prognosticate of our separation from the See of Rome, which then chanced by a spaniel of the Earl of Wiltshire, which came out of England with him, and stood directly between the Earl and the Bishop of Rome, when the said Bishop had advanced forth his feet to be kissed. Now whether the spaniel perceived the Bishop's foot of another nature than it ought to be, and so taking it to be some kind of repast—or whether it was the will of God to show some token by a dog unto the bishop of his inordinate pride, that his feet were more meet to be bitten of dogs than kissed of Christian men—the spaniel...went directly to the Pope's feet, and not only kissed the same unmannerly, but as some plainly reported and affirmed, took fast with his mouth the great toe of the Pope, so that in haste he pulled in his glorious feet from the spaniel: whereat our men, smiling in their sleeves, what they thought God knoweth." (Foxe)

20. Some say, Skye terrier.

21. *Johnson's Dictionary*

22. "The judges made a display of their knowledge of pugs by sending Roderick out of the ring, disqualifying him for 'carrying his tail on the wrong side'" (Dr. Cryer)

23. Short-nosed lap Spaniels were not known in England till the last century.

24. "The Andalusian, or Alicant Dog, has the short muzzle of the pug with the long hair of the spaniel" (William Youatt: *The Dog,* 1845).

25. Other Italian names are: *scimmiotto* (little monkey) and *fancuullino* (little child).

26. According to Philip W. Sergeant, in his *Empress Josephine, Napoleon's Enchantress,* Fortuné belonged to her before her imprisonment, and was introduced into the prison as a bearer of secret messages, which he carried under his collar.

27. The grief at the loss of Fortuné is described by Philip W. Sergeant as follows:
    "Only one blow seems to have come to lessen her happiness—the death of Fortuné. This little pug-dog, whom Napoleon once told Arnault that he found in possession of Madame's bed when he married, and who showed his resentment at the intruder by taking a piece out of his leg, did not limit his hostility to men. He met the cook's dog in the garden at Montebello, and treating him like Napoleon, found him far from equally complacent. The result was that Fortuné was discovered dead. 'It is a most tragic death,' writes Arnault. 'I leave you to imagine what was his Mistress's grief. The Conqueror of Italy could not but show his sympathy. He mourned sincerely for an accident which left him sole possessor of his wife's bed.' But Josephine consoled herself. She 'did as many a woman does to comfort herself for the loss of a lover; she took another.' And Fortuné never lacked a successor during the lifetime of Josephine."

28. Maltese were known as "the lion-dog," but he has mentioned this. Possibly he means the Pekin spaniel.

29. The present Hon. Secretary is Miss E. D. Gilpin, The Hague, Hanworth Road, Hounslow.

30. The Pug-Dog Club, The London and Provincial Pug Club (now amalgamated with The Pug-Dog Club), The Northern Pug Club, which is still in existence, and The Scottish Pug-Dog Club.

31. Belonging to Mr. Foster, and winner of the first prize at Birmingham in 1877.

32. I regret I have been unable to reproduce the photo of the contortionist, so I hopefully leave its diverting antics to the imagination of the reader.

33. Should Mr. Trapman desire a pseudonym for the second edition of his book, might I suggest, "The Man: Pug's Worst Friend!"

34. Joyce, *South American Archaeology.*

The Pug Handbook

*Giving the Origin and History
of the Breed, Its Show Career,
Its Points and Breeding*

by

Wilhelmina Swainston-Goodger

The Goya painting of the Marquessa de Pontejos with her Pug.

Preface

UGS, like all articles of first-rate quality, do not inspire neutral feelings: people either adore or detest them. This may account for the remarkable see-saw of fashion with regard to the breed. In England, in the mid eighteenth century, Pugs were the darlings of royalty and few ladies of fashion were seen without one. By the early nineteenth century they have almost vanished, and one writer pronounced a long epitaph beginning, 'perhaps in the whole catalogue of the canine species there is not one of less utility or possessing less the power of attraction than the pug dog'. In the second half of the century Pugs are popular again—'everywhere in town and country these animals swarm'—and the many distinguished owners are headed by Queen Victoria. The present century seems to be repeating the same pattern: at first with the revulsion against all things Victorian, Pugs, quite unjustly identified with the regime, once more dwindled, but today such differing arbiters of contemporary taste as Mr. Cecil Beaton and Mr. Gilbert Harding choose Pugs for their pets, and you cannot go far in Mayfair without encountering some exquisitely dressed lady accompanied by a beautiful fawn Pug. And so it goes on—no

doubt in future years, when the Atomic Age seems as quaint and old-fashioned as the Victorian Age does to us, people will still be discovering with joy and surprise the peculiar charm and quality of the Pug.

What is this quality? It is not, as one might imagine, something so refined and delicate that only the most fastidious can appreciate it. Remember that the Pug is largest of all the so-called 'toy' dogs and when given half a chance can be as sporting as any small Terrier. In the official Standard the Pug is referred to as 'multum in parvo', and though this strictly only describes his appearance I like to translate it as 'the little dog that has so much'. From his distant Chinese ancestry he inherits an Oriental courtesy and good temper which makes him, for instance, the ideal companion for children, but his long acclimatization in Europe has completely removed the unattractive Oriental 'snootiness' and condescension towards human kind that one finds in some cats. Instead, he has learnt humility and devotion although his aristocratic connections prevent him ever falling to the opposite extreme of sloppy, liquid-eyed servility.

If you have ever lived with a Pug and feel tempted to make his further acquaintance, then do not delay—go out as soon as you can and get one. As you gradually become accustomed to the peculiar charm of the breed, subtle yet full of fun and high spirits, dignified yet utterly loving and trustful, you will soon realize that you could not have made a better investment.

I wish I could here thank individually all the people who have helped me with this book, but I must be content with a general expression of gratitude, with particular mention of all those breeders who kindly lent me photographs and pictures for reproduction; Mr. Clifford Hubbard, who apart from his editorial help has let me have the benefit of his unrivaled knowledge of all things canine; and my son, William, who assisted me with much research and in many other practical ways.

WILHELMINA SWAINSTON GOODGER

CHALFONT ST. PETER, *October, 1958*

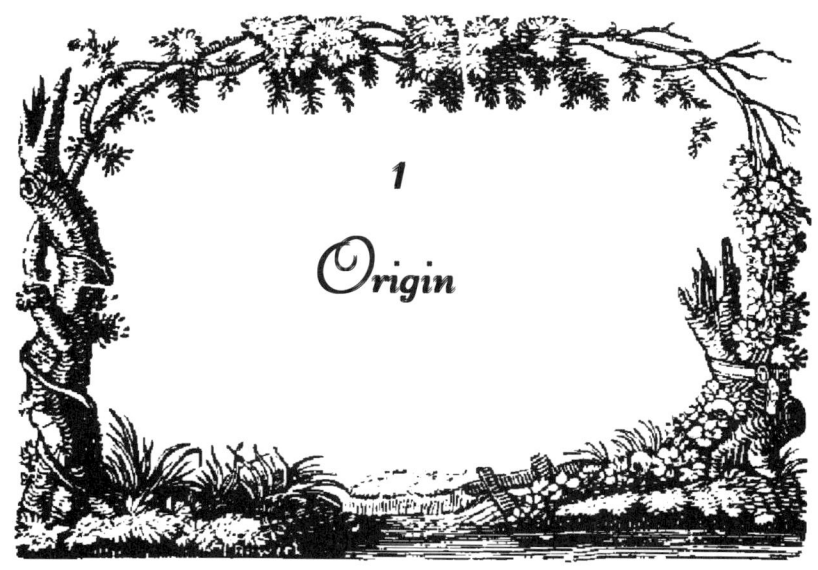

1
Origin

 ET US start with the name 'Pug dog', partly because some solemn nonsense has been written about its derivation, and partly because the word itself is a pointer to the origin of the breed.

The word 'Pug' was in common use here from at least the second half of the sixteenth century, but the first clear identification of the word with a dog does not occur until 1731 when Bailey wrote in his Dictionary, 'Pug a Nickname for a Monkey or Dog'. Prior to that time the word is chiefly used either as a term of endearment, e.g.:

> I have had four husbandes myselfe. The first I called sweet duck: the second, deare heart, the third, pretty pugge. (Sir G. Carey, 1580)

or as meaning a puck or imp as:

> Devils in Sarmatia honoured, called Kottri or Kibaldi, such as we Pugs or Hobgoblins call (Heywood, 1635)

or later to mean a small pet monkey:

> The Monkey by chance came jumping out with them . . . Poor Pug was had before his betters. (Crull, 1698)

From the late seventeenth century onwards, until the time when 'Pug' became 'Pug dog', the meaning 'pet monkey' prevails, and continues even as late as Samuel Johnson: ' Pug—a kind name of a monkey ' (Johnson's Dictionary). 'Idstone' (Rev. Pearce), a Victorian writer on dogs who, according to Dalziel, 'travels miles out of his way to drag in a fanciful or obscure word or meaning', learnedly derives 'Pug' from the Greek whence comes the Latin *Pugnus* (a fist) because the shadow of a clenched fist was considered to resemble the dog's profile.

It seems unlikely that a word first used to mean a dog in the eighteenth century was derived from the Latin, still less from the Greek, and anyone who has studied pictures of Pugs around this period (or the many Pugs represented in Meissen porcelain made at this time) will not be surprised to find that a word previously used to mean a small monkey comes to be applied to the Pug dog. Though it may horrify modern breeders, who are much concerned to avoid the 'monkey-face', there is no doubt that these early Pugs with their cropped ears, bulging foreheads and shortish muzzles have a strong superficial resemblance to the 'marmouselle' which Cotgrave calls 'a little puppie, or pug to play with'. I wrote just now that the derivation of 'Pug' meaning 'Pug dog' would give us a pointer to the dog's origin, and this is the moment to establish an extremely important point. The early Pug appearance, whose monkey-like resemblance led to the word 'Pug' (monkey) being applied to the breed, was anatomically quite unique among all breeds known in Europe, except for a few stray importations, prior to the first arrival of Pekingese and Japanese Spaniels in the late nineteenth century.[1] By 'quite unique' I mean that the bone structure of the skull of the pure bred Pug has certain peculiarities which are not shared by any other breed (including the Bulldog, and other short-faced Bull breeds), but which are found only in the Oriental short-faced Toys such as the Pekingese, Japanese Spaniel, Ha-pa dog (in the European sense) and, of course, the Lo-sze or Chinese Pug, of which more later.

Anyone who has studied old pictures of Pugs, particularly English ones, might query the above statement on the grounds that many of these pictures resemble small Mastiffs or Bulldogs more than they do the Oriental Toys. Look for example at Buffon's Pug, 1750, and Reinagle's beautifully drawn Pugs of 1805. This query brings us up against the curse of cross breeding, which has left its mark on the breed all over Europe, although attempts to breed back to the original Chinese type during the last hundred years or so have done much to remedy the situation. Sydenham Teak Edwards tells us in his *Cynographia Britannica* (1800) that Pugs were previously crossed with Bulldogs in order to shorten the faces of the latter. There were very much larger Pugs then, he informs us, and a careful study of Reinagle's picture confirms that even in 1805 there were two sizes of Pug, since the smaller (and more Puglike) of the two dogs is clearly an adult and not a puppy. I am in-

Le Doguin, by F. Chereau, 1790, after Buffon.

Detail from a painting by P. Reinagle, 1805. Note the cropped ears.

debted to Miss Veldhuis, of Arnhem, who has made a special study of old German and Dutch dog books, and who informs me that in Germany the Pug was cross-bred with the Pinscher (not the Dobermann, which is a modern development, but the old German Pinscher) in the eighteenth century, again in order to achieve the shorter face in the latter.

It is therefore safe to assume that the traces of Mastiffs, Bulldogs and even Terriers (see an extraordinary so-called Pug depicted in *The Sporting Magazine,* 1789) found in early Pug pictures, about which 'Stonehenge' (J. H. Walsh) is still complaining in 1859, are due to the use of the Pug, the only naturally short-faced dog known in Europe at that time, in crossbreeding to shorten the muzzles of other canine types.

Genuine Meissen porcelain, as produced in the first half of the eighteenth century, gives us example after example of the pure bred Pug type.[2] Another example of the almost pure type, from Spain this time, occurs in Goya's exquisite portrait of the Marquesa de Pontejos, c.1785 (see *Frontispiece*). A third English example is Hogarth's early 'House of Cards,' probably the first extant European picture of a black Pug, which shows that the small goggle-eyed Pug could be found in England as early as 1730, in sharp contrast to Hogarth's own Pug, a mongrel if ever there was one.

A pair of Meissen China Pugs (c. 1730) by J. J. Kaendler.

The *House of Cards,* by William Hogarth, 1730, showing a black Pug. This dog was probably the pet of the children of the first Earl of Pomfret.

THE PUG SKULL

It is important to note that all the Pugs just referred to, though accurately described as short-faced, have by no means the noseless, flat muzzle to which the best modern selective breeding has accustomed us. But the slightly pointed muzzle found here is anatomically quite different from the long, blunt muzzle of the Mastiff, and is quite inconsistent with the peculiarities of bone structure I referred to previously.

It is necessary to explain in rather more detail the differences between the 'normal'[3] type of dog and the Pug type. It is a fact that allowing for variations of type within the breeds themselves, it is next to impossible to distinguish the bare skulls of the Pug, the Pekingese and the Japanese Spaniel. An interesting paper among the *Proceedings* of the Zoological Society for 1867, on 'The Skull of the Chinese Pug-nosed Lapdog', by Dr. J. E. Gray, F.R.S., contains beautifully accurate drawings of the skull of a dog described as a 'Pug' and sent from Japan to the British Museum by Dr. W. Lockhart.

It would be tempting to assume without more ado that the skull depicted in Dr. Gray's paper is a Pug, but internal evidence suggests it may in fact have been a Japanese Spaniel—as mentioned earlier, at this date Pekingese and Japanese Spaniels were quite unknown as distinct breeds in Britain, and were wrongly called 'Peking Pugs' or 'Japanese Pugs'. The drawings referred to almost exactly resemble the official Pug skull held by The Natural History Museum which I have seen and examined, and Dr. Lockhart's scientific description of his skull will do quite as well as a description of any well-bred Pug skull: 'The skull is peculiar for the very large size, broad ventricose and subcubical form of the brain-case, for the great shortness of the face, and the shelving, almost horizontal position of the nasal apertures; the bones of the face are regular, symmetrical; the forehead rather concave.'

One has only to compare the photographs of the Bulldog and Mastiff skulls to see how radically they differ from the Pug skull (which is why a Bulldog's eyes are smaller and wide apart, as opposed to the prominent and more frontally placed goggles of Pug or Pekingese)—notice that the top sides of the cranium appear to be broken off like horns, quite unlike the perfect downward curve of the sides of the Pug skull. In the profile photograph the extraordinary distortion of the Bulldog's jaws, as opposed to the Pug's muzzle, is very clearly shown; bearing in mind the fact that Bulldogs were a Mastiff type dog deliberately bred shortfaced, we see that though the upper jaw has been retracted by breeding, the lower jaw is still a normal, long-faced dog's, which has curved upwards, instead of remaining straight, thus producing the familiar undershot appearance peculiar to the Bull breeds.

In the Pug or Pekingese or Japanese Spaniel, on the other hand, the jaw structure is comparatively light and most of the bone structure of the head goes into the characteristically curved cranium.

It is easy to see, and important to note, that a Pug could have a muzzle as long as, say, a Cavalier King Charles Spaniel[4] without losing the essential features which distinguish its skull from the Mastiff or Bulldog type. In fact, many of the representations of Victorian and older Pugs (as in some Meissen figures) show dogs with longish muzzles but which retain the bulging forehead and goggle eyes which are completely foreign to the Mastiff and Bulldog, and are only found in that Oriental prototype of which the Pug, Pekingese and Japanese Chin are three different developments.

It is sometimes suggested that the extreme differences between the Pug and Mastiff heads are explicable on the grounds that if you deliberately set out to breed a short-faced dog from a long-faced one the skull is bound to be modified in the way the Pug skull differs from that of the 'normal' dog skull. But the facts do not bear this out. For many centuries attempts have been

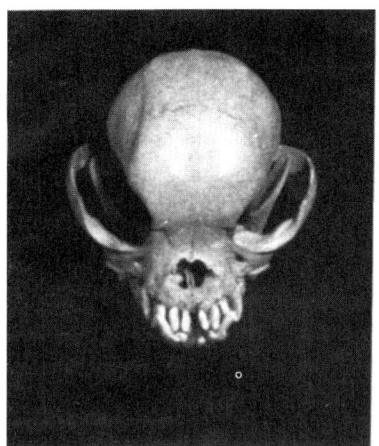 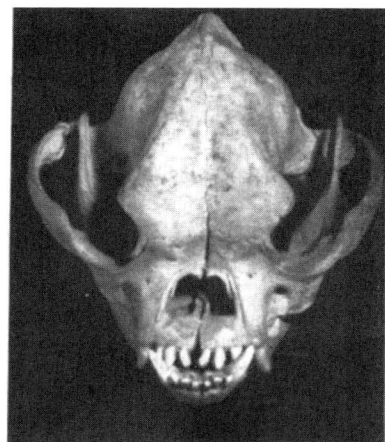

Cranial comparisons of the Pug and the Bulldog. On the left is the frontal aspect of a Pug skull and on the right we see the frontal aspect of a Bulldog skull.

made to produce a short-faced dog from the Mastiff type, the Bulldog, and the result is a dog which, in spite of its short face, has essentially the 'normal' type skull with the flat cranium and preponderance of bone in the jaws. Exactly the same is found in the shortfaced 'Bull' derivations, the Boxer, French Bulldog and the Boston Terrier, though the latter breed, having by careful selective breeding remained nearer to the Bull Terrier than to the Bulldog, has the even and not undershot muzzle. The only occasions when the skulls of short-faced breeds tend to resemble that of the Pug rather than the 'normal' type of skull, are those where

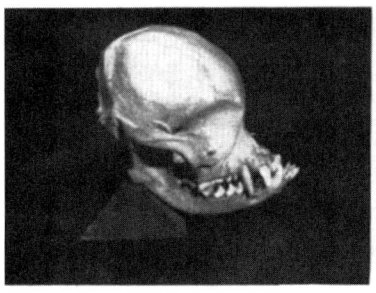 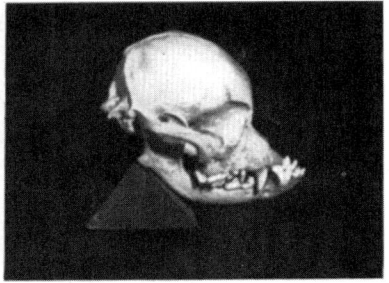

Cranial comparisons of a Pug and Pekingese skull. On the left is the lateral aspect of a Pug skull; on the right is the same view of a Pekingese skull.

there has been a definite cross-breeding with dogs of Pug type, and the Pug physiognomy has prevailed, as in such comparatively recent developments as the Griffon Bruxellois and the short-faced King Charles Spaniel. One or two French Bulldogs also show distinct traces of Pug crosses, though I suggest such dogs are as impure specimens of their own breed as those early Pugs with narrow foreheads and undershot muzzles were of theirs.

This examination of the skulls of the Pug, Mastiff and Bulldog has been necessary because of an unfortunate tendency among certain writers to classify Pugs in the Mastiff class and with the Bull breeds. Based on some loose remarks by E. C. Ash, and on the undoubted resemblances to the Mastiff type caused by latent traces of the Bulldog crosses which occurred in the eighteenth and again in the nineteenth centuries, this classification has been followed by some modern writers. It is not justified by the evidence; and I hope future writers who attempt classification will replace the Pug in the Oriental short-faced Toy Dog class to which its skull shows it belongs.

What are the alleged resemblances of the Mastiff to the Pug? A short, blunt muzzle? But strip both breeds down to the skull and you will see that the relation and shape of cranium and facial structure are fundamentally different. Fawn colour, with black mask, and having wrinkle about the face, found in both breeds? But early pictures of Mastiffs [e.g. those of Buffon (1750), Bewick (1790), Reinagle (1805), and Howitt 1809)] show that

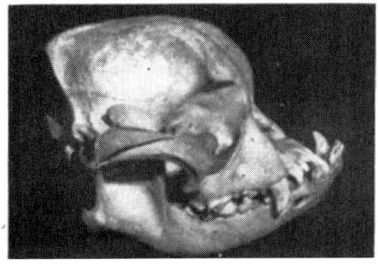 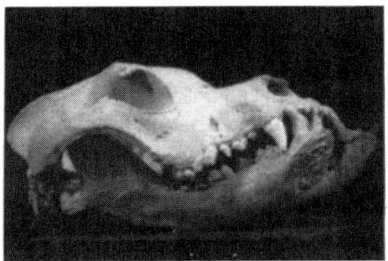

The lateral aspect of a Bulldog skull is shown on the left. A Mastiff skull appears on the right.

the breed was only beginning to emerge as a distinct breed (rather than a general type) in the late eighteenth century, and the dogs shown are not fawn in colour nor have they wrinkles; Pugs, on the other hand, were fawn with black masks, and fully individual, at least as far back as the early eighteenth century.

It does not therefore seem feasible that the Pug could have developed from the Mastiff, since unless the Mastiff had been crossed with some other breed with the peculiar head structure of the Pug, that head structure would not have emerged. As we have seen, at the time when Pugs in Europe were already fully individual, there was no other dog with the bulging forehead and weak muzzle of the Meissen dogs, and so such crossings could not have taken place.

Moreover in the early eighteenth century, the Mastiff, as distinct from the Great Dane, Bulldog, Newfoundland, etc., could hardly be said to exist in England as an individual and separate breed, so theories based on resemblances between the modern Mastiff and the Pug have no sound basis.[5]

If the Pug did not develop from the Mastiff, or from any other known European breed, what was its origin, and how did it get to Europe? We cannot place much reliance on theories contained in books on dogs written before *The Dog in Health and Disease* by 'Stonehenge' (J. H. Walsh) was published in 1859. All the same, it is interesting to note the uncertainty of earlier authorities.

Considering the sorry traces of cross-breeding, and the rarity of the pure Pug type, one would not be surprised to find them all deriving the Pug from the Bulldog or Mastiff, and claiming it as an English breed.[6] In fact, we get a variety of views. Buffon (1750) (who thought swallows kept warm in winter by flying to the bottom of a lake), makes a characteristic guess that the Pug is a Bulldog modified by a hot climate, i.e. by the Dutch in South Africa. Taplin (1805) quotes theories that the Pug first came from 'Muscovy' (Russia), that it is indigenous to Holland or that it is a cross between the Bulldog and the Little Dane. Smith (1843), following earlier writers, mentions four types of Pug: Roquet, Artois Mongrel, Little Danish Dog, and Alicant; of these the first two are French, and the last, which has 'a Puglike muzzle and the coat of a Water Spaniel', is Spanish. Some of these 'Pugs' are illustrated by Buffon and show only too clearly the dire effects of crossbreeding. One writer, so long ago as 1786, shows no uncertainty as to the origin of the Pug. This is Dr. Johnson's witty friend Mrs. Thrale who, under her later married name of Piozzi, published in 1789 her *Journal of Travels Through Italy, France and Germany*. Apropos of Italy, she mentions that: 'A transplanted Hollander, carried thither originally from China, seems to thrive particularly well in this part of the world, the little Pug dog or Dutch Mastiff.'

China, Russia, Holland, Spain, Denmark and South Africa—our older authorities are anything but unanimous. After 1850, when shows and selective breeding first began to flourish, the field had narrowed down, in the minds of the chief Pug breeders of the time (so Mr. Reginald Mayhew tells us), to three: China, Russia, Holland. 'Stonehenge' writing in 1859, refers to recent Pug-Bulldog crosses, and complains of the harm done to the Pug by 'impure blood creeping out... showing evil evidence of the crosses which have taken place'. These evidences are significantly, 'yellow masks, low foreheads and pointed noses'. No wonder the leading breeders of the time decided to try and introduce pure stock from the fountainhead.

EARLY IMPORTATIONS

Lord Willoughby de Eresby managed to obtain two Russian Pugs from a lady tight-rope walker named Blondin, and Mrs. Mayhew commenced a Chinese strain with her famous dog "Click", the son of "Lamb" and "Moss", two Chinese Pugs. Mr. Mayhew, her son, writes as follows:

> "Click"'s parents—"Lamb" and "Moss"— were Chinese beyond dispute. They were captured in the Emperor of China's palace during the siege of Peking in 1867 or 1868, and were brought to England by the then Marquis of Wellesley, I think. Anyhow, they were given to a Mrs. St. John, who brought them several times to our house. Alike as two peas, they were solid apricot fawn, without a suspicion of white; had lovely heads and expressions; but unlike their son, they were close to the ground and a shade long in body. (Watson, *The Dog Book.*)

Some of the less important details here seem inaccurate. The siege of Peking was in 1860, not 1867, and the last Marquis of Wellesley died in 1842. However, Lord John Hay,[7] who brought the first Pekingese back from the siege, was a kinsman of the Wellesley family by marriage. After 1860 British troops remained in the country, and Dr. Rennie, an army surgeon, tells us that many short-faced Toy Dogs were stolen from the common people by the soldiers. He himself purchased one of these, a cross between a Pug and a King Charles Spaniel, at the Lung Fu Sse Market for two and a half dollars, another going for twenty dollars.[8] One would not expect Dr. Rennie, still less the troops, to distinguish between the various Chinese breeds: Pekingese, the short-haired Ha-pa and the Pug or Lo-sze, and "Lamb" and "Moss" were probably either bought or stolen in China, very likely around 1867[9] by some soldier or member of the Embassy staff and then bought back to England.

If the first Pekingese were arriving in England at this time, and no one had seen this strange new breed before, is it possible that "Lamb" and "Moss" were not Pugs, but Pekingese? Mr. Mayhew describes them as being low in body and as rough-coated as a roughhaired Fox Terrier, and E. C. Ash, misinterpreting these words, calls "Lamb" 'long-haired'. However, if you look at the portrait of "Click", the son of "Lamb" and "Moss" you will see that this is not the progeny of Pekingese but a true and beautiful Pug, and that the coat, though it may be 'rough,' is not 'long'.

Most of the prominent English Pugs from 1875 to 1895 trace to "Click", and, as Mr. Watson reminds us, all the good American Pugs from 1880 to 1900 also trace to ' "Click", a dog of pure Chinese stock'.

This Chinese strain, which did so much to bring the Pug back to type, was later reinforced when Lady Brassey brought back a number of black Pugs direct from China after one of her visits to the Far East in her yacht, the 'Sunbeam'; some of these dogs and their progeny were shown at Maidstone Show in 1886 and caused something of a furor. Lady Brassey is reticent in her published writings about how and where she got her original black Pugs, and this led to unfounded suspicions that they never came from China at all. I am indebted to Mrs. Pryor, who has described conversations she had with Captain Maudsley, Lady Brassey's godson, who died some years ago at the age of eighty. He well remembered Lady Brassey's return from China with several black

Miss Deady Keane's "Pekinese Pugs"

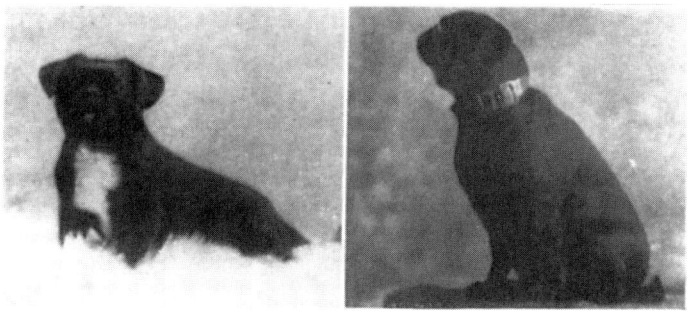

Mrs. E. B. Guyer's "Kreuger," a Chinese import and the black English-bred Pug, "Bon Bon."

Pugs which she told him she had obtained there. One of them she gave to him, but it was unfortunately later stolen.

A few years later, Mrs. Eva B. Guyer of Philadelphia imported both black and chestnut-and-white Pugs from China to America, where they gave support to the reversion to the Chinese type which the prevalence of the "Click" strain among Pugs exported to America had already set in motion. It is interesting to note that the blacks imported from China by Lady Brassey and by Mrs. Guyer all tended to show traces of white on the chest and on the paws. This fault, which occasionally recurs in both fawns and blacks today, is still known among older breeders as 'the mark of China'.

In China, as we shall see in the next chapter, Pugs were bred in all colours, but the most popular colour at the time, as with the Pekingese, appears to have been chestnut-brindle-and-white. If you study the 'Pekinese Pugs' and Mrs. Guyer's black below, you will see that in spite of the difference in colours, and the various unavoidable traces of cross-breeding which still mark the European Pug, there can be no reasonable doubt that the Chinese Pug and the European Pug are one and the same breed.

When the Chinese strain was first established, and Chinese Pugs, fawn and black, were first directly imported to England in the late nineteenth century, the mystery that had puzzled older writers on dogs—where and how did this unusual breed originate?—became a mystery no longer. Collier, in his scholarly *Dogs of China and Japan,* 1921, showed from original sources, written and pictorial, that the Chinese Pug or Lo-sze was established as an individual breed long before Pugs made their first appearance in Europe. Gradually the more scientific canine historians one by one pronounced that the theory of Chinese origin was the most convincing. Watson, Leighton, Ash, Croxton Smith, and Clifford Hubbard have all given their support to the theory.

One last query remains. If Pugs originated in the Far East, how did they get to Europe so early, from so far away? The Roman poet Grattius (before A.D. 9) describes in his *Cynegeticon Liber* various foreign types of dog, and remarks: "some prefer to breed Chinese dogs, a race of implacable anger'. This shows that Chinese dogs were known in Rome at the time of the life of Christ.[10] The first Pug clearly recorded in European history is the famous dog who saved the life of William the Silent by barking and warning him of a night attack by the Spanish in 1572. Pugs as a result became national heroes in Holland for well over a hundred years afterwards. Since the Dutch were not trading regularly with China until 1604, it seems unlikely that William's Pug was obtained by them direct. The Portuguese were trading at Canton from 1516 however, so William, who held high rank under the Spanish Government before the War, probably obtained his unusual pet from a Spanish or Portuguese source.

In 1888, when the site of the old Post Office in London was being excavated, the remains of an old Roman villa came to light, and among them was found the skull of a 'small, short-faced dog', Perhaps this was the first English Pug, brought over here by the Romans! All the same, Grattius' description of the Chinese dogs known to the Romans as ' a race of implacable anger' seems quite inappropriate to the courteous and well-tempered Pug dog.

2
History

HE Pug has had a long and interesting history in most civilized parts of the world. In the space at my disposal I can only give some brief glimpses of that history, starting with China which, as I have argued in the first chapter, was almost certainly the country in which the common ancestor of the Pug, the Pekingese and Japanese Spaniel first developed.

CHINA

Dogs were known and respected in China from very early times. As far back as 1115 B.C. the 'Chancien' or Dog-feeder was an established official post; this was apparently the first dog judge, since part of his work was 'to judge the quality and character of different dogs from their appearance'. An 800 B.C. 'Book of Rites' divides dogs into three classes: hunting-dogs, water-dogs and edible dogs; and in 700-600 B.C. we get the first reference to 'short-mouthed' dogs which were evidently admired[11] since they were conveyed in carriages which were specially prepared for them. These were sporting dogs rather than Toys, as we are told 'the purpose of providing carriages for them is to preserve their energy before arriving at the hunting-place'.

The first clear reference to a dog which is both shortfaced and small occurs in A.D. 732 when a 'Ssuchuan pai dog' was among the tributes sent from a Korean State to Japan. The word 'pai' at this time indicated a short-faced dog with short legs which was small enough to go under the low tables around which the Chinese sat on mats. An important town in the Province of Ssuchuan is Lo-Chiang, and the Ssuchuan pai dog from about A.D. 950 onwards was more precisely referred to as the 'Lo-Chiang-sze' or 'Lo-Chiang'. The suffix '-sze' was commonly tacked on to Ssuchuan place names, and at a later date 'Lo-Chiang-sze' was contracted into 'Lo-sze' which, up to forty years ago, was the Chinese name for the Pug.

Lo-szes were very popular during this period and particularly during the great Sung dynasty (A.D. 969-1153). A famous one is described as follows:

> About the year A.D. 990 an offcial in Ssuchuan gave the Emperor T'ai Tsung a Lo-Chiang dog named T'ao Hua (peach-flower). It was extremely small and very intelligent. It followed the Emperor everywhere. When there was an audience the dog preceded him, and by its bark announced the

Chinese Pug from an Imperial Dog Book, with another painting by Tsou Yi-Kwei (1686-1766).

Emperor's arrival. When the Emperor died the dog manifested its sorrow with tears and whining. The palace eunuchs endeavoured to train the dog to precede the new Emperor, but without success. The Emperor caused to be made an iron cage with white cushions in sign of mourning, and this, containing the dog, was carried in the Imperial chair to his master's tomb. There the dog died, and the Emperor Chen Tsung (a faithful disciple true to the Confucian doctrine) issued a decree ordering it to be wrapped in the cloth of an Imperial umbrella and buried alongside of its master.

Dogs seem to have gone somewhat out of fashion after the Sung dynasty, and during Ming times (fourteenth and fifteenth centuries) cat breeding was all the rage. By the beginning of the sixteenth century, however, references to dogs in Chinese literature again become frequent. European trade with China, which had been virtually discontinued for centuries, first resumed on any scale when the Portuguese began trading at Canton in 1516; as suggested earlier it is probable that small Chinese dogs brought to Europe at this time may well have been not only the progenitors of the European Pug but also of the Toy Spaniels which now begin to appear in the sixteenth century Italian paintings.

From the late seventeenth century date the first of the Imperial dog books which are still extant. These books, whose illustrations were made by court painters, were intended to set standards for the various breeds, and were kept currently up to date at the Imperial Palace in Peking until the early part of the present century. As breeding precedents one would expect the pictures to be realistic, but the earlier ones, at any rate, are stylised in the Chinese manner, and it would be unwise to regard them as exact representations of the breeds in question. Collier reproduces two beautiful colour plates by Tsou Yi-Kwei (1686-1766), one showing a Pekingese and the other a Pug. Though the Pug has been clearly bred small to the 'sleeve dog' specification, it is still unmistakably of the same breed as the 'Pekinese Pugs.'[12]

In 1860, when British soldiers sacked the Imperial Palace, and the years following, dogs of the Pekingese and Pug type began to trickle back to Europe from China for the first time in any numbers since the early sixteenth century. As explained previously, it was towards the end of this decade that the two Chinese Pugs "Lamb" and "Moss" appeared in England and, through their son "Click" initiated the return of the original type which was so badly needed after centuries of cross-breeding with all and sundry. This regression to the original type was further assisted by the import of black Pugs from China by Lady Brassey.

A head study of Mrs. Mayhew's "Click."

In China, the breeding of Toy dogs probably achieved its greatest precision during the reign of the redoubtable Empress Tsu Hsi, known to history as 'Old Buddha'.[13] Up to the death of the Empress in 1908 there were seldom less than one hundred dogs in the Imperial Kennels, and scrolls from the Imperial dog books of the time distinguish clearly between the short-coated Lo-szes and the longcoated Pekingese.

It is noticeable that all the Lo-szes in the old Chinese paintings have the apparently flat Pug head whereas the Pekingese and Ha-pas shown in these paintings are distinguished from the Lo-szes (unlike modern Pekingese) by their round, domed skulls.

After the death of 'Old Buddha' breeding to type in China languished, and anyone who travels to China today in search of pure Pugs or Pekingese is likely to meet blank incomprehension. China and Japan therefore owe a great debt to the British and American breeders who have presented and cultivated the Chinese Pug, Pekingese and Japanese Spaniel, and saved these exquisite breeds from extinction.

I will conclude this section by giving some interesting notes on the differences between the Pekingese and Pug (Lo-sze) as they were developed in China. This information was supplied to Collier by Wang Hou-Chun, who had seventy-five years' experience as a keeper of dogs in the Palace of Prince Wu Yeh.

> One of the most important characteristics of the Chinese Lo-sze dog is, in addition to universal shortness of coat, elasticity of skin existing in far greater degree than with the 'Pekingese'. The point most sought after by Chinese breeders was the 'Prince' mark, formed by the wrinkles on the forehead with a vertical bar in imitation of the Chinese character for 'Prince'. This same character is distinguished by the Chinese in the stripes on the forehead of the tiger, which, in consequence, is the object of superstitious veneration among the ignorant. The button, or white blaze, on the forehead was also encouraged in the Lo-sze dog, but was not of the same importance as the wrinkles. Other points, such as compactness of body, flatness of face, squareness of jaw and soundness of bone, are similar to those of the 'Pekingese', except as regards the ears, which were small and likened to a dried half apricot set with the outer face on the side of the head and pointing slightly backwards. The 'Chiaotzu', or horn-ear, is also admissible. The legs are but slightly bent at the elbow. The tail is docked by the Chinese, with a view to symmetrical form. The curly tail, however, is known to have existed ('sze Kuochu-erh'), and the double curl was also known.

EUROPE

The first European Pug to which we have clear reference is one of the most famous of all, the dog already mentioned who saved the life of William the Silent at Hermigny when the Spanish made a surprise night attack on the Dutch camp on 11th Sep-

A painting by J. C. Bell, c. 1845.

tember, 1572. Here is Sir Roger Williams' account, from his *Actions of the Lowe Countries,* 1618:

'For I heard the Prince say often, that as hee thought, but for a dog he had been taken. The Camisado was given with such resolution, that the place of armes took no alarme, untill these fellowes were running in with the enemies in their tailes. Whereupon the dogge, hearing a great noyse, fell to scratching and crying, and withall leapt on the Prince's face, awaking him being asleep, before any of his men. And albeit the Prince lay in his armes, with a lackey alwaies holding one of his horses ready bridled; yet at the going out of his tent, with much adoe he recovered his horse before the enemie arrived. Nevertheless one of his Quiries was slaine taking horse presently after him; and divers of his servants were forced to escape amongst the guards of foote, which could not recover their horses. For truth ever since, untill the Prince's dying day, he kept one of that dog's race; so did many of his friendes and followers. The most of all of these dogs were white little houndes, with crooked noses,[14] called Camuses.' (Camus is a French word meaning 'snub-nosed'.)

This signal blow for the Reformation, whose fate was then in the balance in Holland, was celebrated for many years afterwards by the Dutch affixing orange coloured ribbons to the collars of their Pugs, treating them as royal favourites. When William of Orange crossed to England to become its King in 1688, with his wife, our Mary II as Queen, the Dutch Pugs with their orange ribbons arrived as an official part of the royal retinue, and the breed soon after became immensely popular in England.

The Frontispiece to this book shows that Pugs, and very pure-bred Pugs too, were known in Spain as early as 1785. An amusing error has led some writers to assume that Pugs were known even earlier than this in Spain, at the Court of Ferdinand and Isabella. This has its source in the name 'Isabellean' which was given to Pugs in France, the word 'Isabella' having reference to the 'soiled calico' colour of the Pug's coat. The French word in fact derives from Isabel of Austria (d. 1633), daughter of Philip II of Spain, who made a famous vow during the Siege of Ostend not to change her linen until the Fort was captured. The Siege lasted three years, hence the meaning given to 'Isabella'! 'Belle' or 'Bella' were common pet names given to Pugs, at any rate throughout the Victorian era, which may have first originated from the breed having once been called 'Isabellean'.

The Pug was certainly known in France in the late seventeenth century, as illustrations show, though the breed was already seriously distorted by cross-breeding. The French name, to this day, for the Pug, 'Carlin,' is interesting since it was taken from the early eighteenth century French actor 'Carlin' who was celebrated for his performances as Harlequin. This shows that not only had the European Pug achieved its characteristic fawn colour by this period, but also its black mask since it was evidently this latter feature that the breed had in common with the Harlequin of Carlin.

Without doubt the most famous French Pug was "Fortune", the Empress Josephine's pet, who upheld the reputation of valour gained for the breed by William the Silent's Pug, by going for Napoleon with his teeth. I quote from Philip W. Sargeant's *Empress Josephine, Napoleon's Enchantress:*

> Only one blow seems to have come to leaven her happiness—the death of "Fortune". This little Pug dog, whom Napoleon once told Arnault that he found in possession of Madame's bed when he married, and who showed his resentment of the intruder by taking a piece out of his leg, did not limit his hostility to men. He met the cook's dog in the garden at Montabello, and treating him like Napoleon, found him far from equally complacent. The result was that "Fortune" was discovered dead. 'It is a most tragic death' writes Arnault, 'I leave you to imagine his Mistress's grief. The Conqueror of Italy could not but show his sympathy. He mourned sincerely for an accident which left him sole possessor of his wife's bed!' But Josephine consoled herself. She did as many a woman does, to comfort herself for the loss of a lover; she took another and "Fortune" never lacked a successor during the lifetime of Josephine.

I have already quoted Mrs. Piozzi on the popularity of Pugs in Italy when she visited that country in 1786; another passage is lively enough to set out here:

> A very vivacious man informed me yester morning, that his poor wife was half broken-hearted at having such a Countess's dog run over; 'for' said he, 'having suckled the pretty creature herself, she loved it like one of her children'. I bid him repeat the circumstances, that no mistake might be made; he did so; but seeing me look shocked, or ashamed, or something he didn't like, 'Why, Madam' said the fellow, 'it is a common thing enough for ordinary men's wives to suckle the lap-dogs of ladies of quality', adding that they were paid for their

milk, and he saw no harm in gratifying one's superiors. As I was disposed to see nothing but harm in disputing with such a competitor, our conference finished soon, but the fact is certain.

The popularity of Pugs in Germany during the early eighteenth century, particularly among the Freemasons in Saxony, has already been mentioned, as has the fact that Pugs were crossbred with Pinschers to shorten the muzzles of the latter.

It is interesting to note that the German names for the Pug, 'Mops' and 'Mopshund,' were derived from the Dutch 'Mopshond', which in turn came from the Dutch word 'Mopperen', to mope, or look peevish.

'Mops' was also used in Germany as a slang expression for a man with a lugubrious countenance.

There is no German word corresponding to 'Mopperen', which strongly indicates that the 'Mops' or 'Mopshund' came from Holland to Germany, as it did to England. In Germany the breed has always retained the Dutch 'Mops', but this name was never used in Britain, as from the time of the Dutch invasion in 1688 it was first called 'Dutch Mastiff', or more commonly 'Dutch Pug', because the wrinkled mask was thought to resemble the Pugs of the day (pet monkeys). When the Pugs ceased to be fashionable the prefix 'Dutch' was dropped, and they began to be called simply 'Pugs', or more correctly 'Pug dogs'.

ENGLAND

It has been suggested both by 'Stonehenge' and, very recently, by Mr. Vesey-FitzGerald, that Pugs were known in England before the seventeenth century. It is likely that an odd Pug or two may have come across from Holland where they were so popular, but there is in fact no positive evidence that the breed had reached England before William of Orange and Mary II brought them across in their retinue in 1688; they are certainly not mentioned in Dr. Caius's famous list of English breeds first published in 1570.

During the eighteenth century Pugs became extremely popular, and around the time of Hogarth, as Rawdon B. Lee says: 'Dutch Pugs were as fashionable as black pages, and no lady of title was considered to be fully equipped unless she had both in her following.' As the Hogarth picture shows, the black Pug had reached England as early as 1730.

Hogarth's own liking for the breed, witnessed by the inclusion of his Pug "Trump" (a deplorable specimen, rightly dubbed 'a mongrel of smooth-coated Terrier design' by Mr. Hubbard in his *Dogs in Britain, 1948),* in the artist's famous self portrait, was seized on by his enemies who 'diverted themselves hugely with fancy representations of 'Painter Pugg', *(William Hogarth,* by Austin Dobson).

The breed reached its peak of popularity during the reign of George III whose wife, Princess Charlotte of Mecklenburg-Strelitz, was devoted to Pugs, and one of them is painted with great care in the well-known portrait of George III at Hampton Court.

George IV kept a Pug, but with the close of the eighteenth century interest in the breed languished, and by 1804 the author of *The Sportsman's Cabinet* is libelling the breed as follows:

> For, perhaps, in the whole catalogue of the canine species, there is not one of less utility, or possessing less the powers of attraction that the Pug dog, applicable to no sport, appropriated to no useful purpose, susceptible of no predominant passion, and in no way whatever remarkable for any extra eminence, he has continued from era to era for what alone he might have been originally intended, the patient follower of a ruminating philosopher, or the adulating and consolatory companion of an old maid.

This seems to have represented the general view, since 'Stonehenge' tells us that up till 1840 the Pug was exceedingly rare. One reason for this was no doubt the increased coarsening of the true type by crossbreeding, lamented by 'Stonehenge' as quoted in my first chapter. In the decade 1840-50, he continues, '.... several admirers of Pugs attempted to breed from good foreign strains', and from then onwards breeders, notably Lord and Lady Willoughby de Eresby, Mr. Morrison and Mrs. Mayhew, laboured valiantly to stop the rot and eradicate as far as possible the false elements of Bulldog and Terrier from the Pug's physiognomy; how this came about I have already described.

Two important strains derive from these pioneer efforts, their chief distinction being one of colour, the 'Willoughby' Pug (later sometimes called 'Pepper and Salt', owing to the black hairs interspersed), and the 'Morrison', a yellow fawn; both these types are clearly recognizable among Pugs of to-day, and each has its individual beauty. The Morrison strain was derived from a Guelph or pure Dutch source, and the Willoughby from the Russian Pugs obtained by Lord Willoughby de Eresby.[15]

By the 1870's Dalziel was able to write that 'the Pug market is overstocked, and everywhere in town and country these animals swarm'. There is no need to expatiate on the immense popularity of Pugs in late Victorian times, a popularity which led to the usual unfavourable reaction when all things Victorian came to be regarded as stuffy and dated. No doubt the habit of many old ladies of giving Pugs no exercise and at the same time cramming them with food until their goggles popped (and Pugs, greediest of dogs, will never stop eating so long as anything edible is within reach) contributed to the unfair impression that all dogs of this breed were fat, immobile, pop-eyed, snorting slugs—well might William the Silent's warrior Pug and Josephine's brave "Fortune" turn in their graves!

The Pug Dog Club was founded on 16th January, 1883, and the Standard

C. Morrison's "Punch" and "Tetty," from an 1879 woodcut.

A lithograph from a sketch by C. Derby of *The Pugs' Tea Party*, given by William Davenport Bromley, in 1850.

which, with minor alterations, is still in use today was adopted on the 26th of that month.

In 1886 at Maidstone Show, Lady Brassey exhibited black Pugs from the strain she had imported direct from China, when a separate class for this variety was first granted. This brings us near enough to the start of the twentieth century during which, particularly since the Second World War, the Pug has once more leapt back into favour among the discriminating. The fact that a fawn Pug, a pet of his daughter Mary when a child, was once an honoured member of Sir Winston Churchill's household is, I think, sufficient answer to the ill-natured cock-a-snooks levelled at the over-fed, pop-eyed monster which so unfairly symbolised the Victorian Pug.

BLACK PUGS

I would like to conclude this chapter with a note on the history of black Pugs, since other writers have gone astray on

Great Exhibition

OF THE

Pugs of all Nations,

AND

Fête given by

William Davenport Bromley, Esq.

THURSDAY, MAY 30TH, 1850.

THERE WHERE PRESENT :—

The Lady Willoughby de Eresby's Mops and Nell

The Honble. Alberic Willoughby's Nina.

The Viscountess Villiers Desdemona.

The Lord Elphinstone's Mungo.

The Honble. Mrs. Cowper's Tim.

Sir Robert Brownrigg's Othello.

Mr. Davenport Bromley's Smut and Juba, &c. &c.

this subject through lack of information. In most dog histories you will read that black Pugs were first introduced to England by Lady Brassey, who brought some back from China after one of her voyages to the Far East in her yacht, the 'Sunbeam'. In an interesting series of articles in the *Ladies' Kennel Journal,* 1895-96, on Queen Victoria's dogs, the anonymous author somewhat indignantly questions this theory, pointing out that black Pugs were known in England long before the Brassey Pugs arrived, that Queen Victoria herself had a black Pug 'the very counterpart of "Jack Spratt", Lady Brassey's first black Pug' when Lady Brassey was a child in the nursery, and further suggesting that Lady Brassey's blacks were bred in this country and never came from China at all.

There is no doubt that Lady Brassey did bring blacks back from China, and there is evidence of other importations of Chinese blacks to England (see Rawdon B. Lee's *Modern Dogs,* Non-Sporting Division pp. 20 *et seq.).* Nor was "Jack Spratt" (also called "Mahdi") Lady Brassey's first black Pug; a stud advertisement in the *Ladies' Kennel Journal* for December, 1894 shows that he was the son, bred in England, of a pair of the original Chinese imports. Moreover, Queen Victoria's black Pug is not good evidence against the theory of importation, since it was admitted in a later issue of the *Ladies' Kennel Journal,* 1896, to have been imported, so it probably came from China as well.[16] The claim that the black Pug was a native English development, which was emphatically set out in a letter to the Kennel Club on 3rd February 1896, applying for separate registration for the black Pug, and signed by Mrs Stennard-Robinson on behalf of fifty-nine breeders and eleven judges, has always seemed to me to lack any firm basis in such evidence as is available. No doubt smutty Pugs had cropped up in litters from time to time; and Mr. Mayhew wrote about the Pugs of his mother's day: 'I have seen so many born practically black in those days, and consigned to the bucket on that account, that I have often marvelled that more recent exhibitors should have been so deluded as to consider the introduction of the black Pug to be a novelty.'

But the beautiful black Pugs seen around the turn of this century (for instance, Miss Jenkinson's "Duke Beira") closely

An 1894 woodcut of Mrs. M. D. Robinson's Nap II, Little Nap, Black Berry and Black Gem.

followed the true Chinese type, and certainly derived from the Brassey Chinese strain.

Be that as it may, it is now no longer possible to maintain that the pure black Pug was unknown in England before the Brassey importations. The early Hogarth painting, dated 1730, remained in obscurity until cleaning revealed the signature of the artist, less than ten years ago; it now belongs to Major The Hon. J. B. Fermor-Hesketh of Cosgrove Hall, by whose kind permission my son was enabled to study the painting. The Pug in the painting is not only jet black, it is also a remarkably true specimen, much nearer to type than the mongrelly fawns portrayed by Hogarth elsewhere: in 'Marriage a la Mode', for example. This proves conclusively that the true black Pug was known in England nearly one hundred and fifty years before the Brassey importations.

Where did the Hogarth black Pug come from? Its trueness of type suggests an imported dog very close to an original Chinese strain. At any rate one can say that black Pugs were very rare indeed in England before the 1880's though there is a doubtful reference to them in Goldsmith's *Animated Nature,* and a more definite one in a veterinary note dated 2nd September, 1843 in Youatt's *The Dog* (1845).

Earlier in this chapter I have quoted Collier to the effect that in China Lo-szes were bred in all different colours, and the illustration from an Imperial dog book shows that all-black Pugs were known there at least as far back as the beginning of the eighteenth century. A son of the King of Siam, who visited an English breeder, Mrs. Crawshay, in 1895, and 'christened' her current litter of black Pugs with suitably fanciful names, informed her that 'black Pugs are Siamese, and the Emperor of China got his from there, but does not allow them to become common in China'.

3
Some Early Show Dogs

TIME and space being available, one could produce a formidable array of Pugs who have distinguished themselves in the show ring, since dog shows first catered for Pugs in 1860 and 1861.

The time we live in being most important to us now, I propose here only to mention some of the most notable Pugs and dogs who have influenced the breed during the last twenty-five years or so.

A well-known breeder and judge was Mrs. Prowett Ferdinands, of 'Prowett' prefix, the blacks being rather her favourites. The Prowett stamp is still to be seen amongst the best Pugs today. Two of her greatest before the last war were Ch. "Prowett Perfection" and Ch. "Prowett Prizepacket". Mrs. Prowett Ferdinands remains adamant today, as she always was, on the subject of size. The Pug is a Toy dog, and must not be too big.

Another famous breeder and judge was the late Mrs. Vincent Curtis of 'Pen' prefix. Her own exquisite little Ch. "My Pretty Jane", was perhaps the most celebrated of her winners, by "Dark Drumcree", out of "Plain Jane". But Mrs. Curtis will ever be remembered in Pug annals, as having bred that mighty black, and supreme brood bitch, Ch. "Miss Penelope of Inver". The best winning black Pugs today can trace their lineage right back to this great doyenne of the breed. She was by "Massa Sambo of Broadway", out of "Miss Penelope". She was purchased from Mrs. Curtis as a puppy by the Misses Hatrick, Campbell and Morrison, 'of Inver' affix, who in those earlier days were specializing in black Pugs. Ch. "Miss Penelope" was dam of six 'Inver' Champions, five of whom were black. Later on, and until the start of the Second World War, this well-known trio of breeders, exhibitors and judges were equally successful with their fawn Pugs. Some of the best known were Ch. "Riggmoneth Rosalind", bred by the late Mrs. R. C. Shaw, and her daughter Ch. 'Mimosa of Inver". Other great 'Inver' bred fawns were Ch. "Dark Dragoon" and Ch. "Dark Demon". The black bitch Ch. "Ainslie of Inver", bred by Miss E. H. McNair, was yet another of their Champions.

The late Mrs. H. C. Lake, 'of Otter' affix, who only died recently, was another unfailing enthusiast for the correct size. This greatly talented lady's opinion may well merit attention, considering she was one, if not the greatest, of our Toy dog specialists. Pugs were not the only Toys in which she specialized, and she brought distinction to each breed she sponsored. As a judge she was always in demand. Two of her most famous Pugs to be remembered are Ch. "Captain Nobbs" and his sire Ch. "Narcissus of Otter", both fawns.

Miss B. Thomson of 'Fairlea' prefix bred some famous Pugs of high merit. Two of her best were Ch. "Fairlea Toy Girl", a fawn, and Ch. "Fairlea Antonia", a black.

During the thirties, it can be said that Mrs. E. M. Power 'of

An 1896 painting of Prince Henry of Battenburg's Pug, by C. Burton Barber.

The Swarland Pugs, **owned by Mrs. Hugh Andrews, as painted by Wilson Hepple, in 1898. They are, from left to right, Tetty, Prince, Ch. Nancy, Ch. Taurus and (lying down) Darius.**

Broadway' affix swept the board. She was fortunate in being able to keep a large number of Pugs at the same time. Some of her most famous dogs were Ch. "Lord Tom Noddy", Ch. "Rajah of Broadway". Ch. "Field Marshall of Broadway", Ch. "Scaramouche of Broadway", Ch. "Nell Gwynne of Broadway", Ch. "Majordomo of Broadway" and Ch. "Marie Rose of Broadway". A popular exhibitor and judge, Mrs. Power came out on the side of the larger Pug, always frankly stating she preferred a good sized Pug.

Three names which will also leave an indelible stamp on the breed for many years to come are Mr. G. W. Kerrod 'of Hopeworth' affix, the late Mrs. R. C. Shaw of 'Riggmoneth' prefix and Mrs. M. E. Nikolin 'of Greengables' affix. Mr. and Mrs. Kerrod were most conscientious breeders. Some of their best were blacks, "Princess Caprice of Hopeworth", "Prempeh of Hopeworth" and "Carlin of Hopeworth", not to mention the fawn "Twinkle of Hopeworth", who later won his title, as likewise did "Prempeh", in the hands of their respective owners. "Carlin of Hopeworth" was a small black dog of exceptional prepotency. He was sire of both "Prempeh" and "Twinkle", who was sold as a puppy to Mrs. E. M. Rose of 'Punchbowl' affix. Mr. Kerrod was yet another enthusiast for the smaller Pug, and wanted it kept as strictly as possible within bounds of the accepted Standard.

Mrs. R. C. Shaw besides having bred Ch. "Riggmoneth Rosamund" and Ch. "Riggmoneth Rosalind," as already stated, was owner of one of the most valuable fawn sires ever to grace any period of Pugdom. This was the fawn "Petty Whin of Baronshalt", and one of the last of the great Pugs by the late Miss Rosa Little. This dog reproduced his exceptional and characteristic head, greater width of muzzle, more face wrinkle, and the over-nose wrinkle which hadn't been seen in Pugs so much until "Petty Whin's" good work became evident. There is no doubt that many of the post-war fawn champions are indebted to "Petty Whin of Baronshalt."

A marvellously compact black dog was Ch. "Roy of Ellerslie", who belonged to Mrs. Meese, whose affix, then 'of Ellerslie', has changed since the war while Mrs. Meese herself has become Mrs. H. Hepburn: her new prefix is 'Phairwin'. Ch. "Roy of Ellerslie" was beautifully small and well built. Mrs.

This colored C. Burton Barber illustration of a Pug, Yorkshire Terrier and Italian Greyhound appeared in Vero Shaw's *Illustrated Book of the Dog*, 1879.

Hepburn is now the popular secretary of The Northern Pug Dog Club.

Mrs. M. E. Nikolin 'of Greengables' affix was a non-exhibitor. She bred quite a number of outstanding Pugs, foremost amongst whom was perhaps the late Miss Gwen Atherton's Ch. "Jacqueline of Cedarwood". "Apollo of Greengables" was another who

Mrs. C. Houlker's Ch. Loris, about 1895.

was exported to Canada by myself, and later won his Canadian Championship. Ch. "Rowena of Greengables" was one of Mrs. Nikolin's latest to distinguish herself. She was owned and jockeyed to fame by Miss M. Masland 'of Masberk' affix, after the last war. Mrs. Nikolin's best Pugs were mostly fawns.

In 1936 I purchased the young black dog "Prempeh of Hopeworth" from Mr. G. W. Kerrod. Later he was mated to my fawn "Giovanna of Swainston", bred by Mrs. Curtis. The breeding of these two Pugs is worth noting. "Prempeh", black, by "Carlin of Hopeworth", out of "Sonoma of Hopeworth", and "Giovanna", fawn, by "Toybell", out of "Plainer Jane". In their first litter of seven, Ch. "ThunderCloud of Swainston" saw the light of day. "Prempeh of Hopeworth", his sire, later won his title, after his famous son "Thunder-Cloud" was a full Champion.

Mrs. V. Graham of 'Edenderry' prefix was responsible for a number of famous Pugs. Chief among them were the blacks, Ch. "Edenderry Daphne", bred by the 'Invers', and her son Ch. "Edenderry Coleman". Other well-known winners of hers about this time were "Edenderry Moriarty", "Edenderry Deirdre", "Edenderry Eilyrhee" and "Edenderry Annie Rooney". The latest who managed to get to the top before the last war was the black Ch. "Edenderry Cuan". Though Mrs. Graham, also one of our best known Pug judges, lived in Ireland at that time, she was untiring in coming over here for most of the English shows. Happily she is now with us in England, for good, we hope, and still going as strong as ever. Her black dog Ch. "Edenderry Barney Campbell" is her first post-war Champion, and our latest dog Champion to date.

The latest bitch to win her title is another black, Miss M. Larter's Ch. "Kate of Rydens", bred by Mrs. W. S. Young, and a sister of Ch. "Kandy of Rydens".

R. H. Moore's drawing of Ch. Duke Beira, with his medals.

The late Mrs. Clara Demaine, wife of well-known all-rounder judge Arthur Demaine, can never be forgotten by anyone in Pugs in those days. She was always in demand as a specialist judge at the leading Championship shows, as also were the services of her famous stud dogs under the prefix 'Dark'. She certainly had a flair for picking a good 'un. Some of her most famous were the earlier Ch. "Dark Ducas", fawn; Ch. "Dark Dickory", black; Ch. "Dark Desmond", black (out of Ch. "Dark Diana"); Ch. "Dark Drummer", black, bred by the late Mrs. Gibson; Ch. "Dark Dragoon", fawn, bred by the 'Invers'; as also were Ch. "Dark Demon", fawn; Ch. "Dark Diamond", black, who was later sold to the late Mrs. M. Jeaffreson 'of Jeffyshill' affix; Ch. "Dark Dragoman", bred by Miss B. Thomson; and Ch. "Dark Drago", black, bred by Mr. and Mrs. J. H. Wakefield 'of Glenva' affix.

Miss Hilda Voy of 'Aucott' affix was well to the fore with some good Pugs, black and fawn. The famous brace of black dogs Ch. "Paul" and Ch. "Peter", both 'of Inver', will always be remembered.

In 1937 I experienced that flash of fortune which sometimes comes to a breeder, by breeding Ch. "Thunder-Cloud of Swainston" in a litter of seven. He was by my black "Prempeh of Hopeworth", who later became a Champion, winning his first

Challenge Certificate after his celebrated son had already got his title. Ch. "Thunder-Cloud" was out of my fawn "Giovanna of Swainston." Still to this day acclaimed the 'Pug of the Century', he was unbeaten by any other dog in his breed, until his ninth year, when he came second and reserve best dog in show at the first post-war Championship show of the Pug Dog Club in 1946. He won five Challenge Certificates, two at Cruft's in 1938 and 1939, and was best Pug in show at both our club shows of those same years. At not quite a year old he won his first Challenge Certificate and Best of Breed at Cruft's, 1938, under the late Mr. Sam Crabtree. On the second day he was made Best Toy Dog of Cruft's, and won the International Toy Dog Trophy. This great distinction has yet to be surpassed by any other Pug. Always an onerous task attempting to describe one's own dog, I leave his prowess to be judged by the show successes in his short career, until the war came to stop him showing, together with his last show-time picture taken in 1939.

The late Mrs. M. Micklem and her partner Miss V. Knowles of 'Bitchet' affix were prominent breeders and exhibitors before the war. Some of their winners were the fawn Ch. "Riggmoneth Rhoda", bred by Mrs. R. C. Shaw, "Pearly Queen", fawn, bred by Miss Mavrogordato, and the great black Ch. "Mandor Susie", bred by Mr. F. Davis. In 1939 I purchased Ch. "Susie" and her kennel mate "Pearly Queen."

Early in the war period two outstanding matings took place, the one fawn, the other black. Both have had a powerful in-

Mrs. E. M Power's Ch. Lord Tom Noddy of Broadway.

fluence on fawn and black Pugs since the war. In fawns, Miss Susan Graham Weall's "Phidgity Paprika", by Ch. "Twinkle of Hopeworth", fawn (out of "Heartsease of Broadway", fawn) was mated to Ch. "Thunder-Cloud of Swainston". In blacks, Mrs. C. Demaine's "Dark Dinah" by "Phidgity Pale Puddies", fawn (out of "Regalia of Hopeworth", black), bred by Mr. G. W. Kerrod, was mated to "Dark Dando", by Ch. "Dark Drago", black (out of "Desni of Greengables", black).

From the "Paprika"/"Thunder-Cloud" mating, Miss Graham Weall bred a litter containing "Phidgity Phlash". This lovely bitch would certainly have got her title had it not been for the war. As it was, she was mated to one of Mrs. Nikolin's dogs, "Tinkerbell of Greengables", a fawn. From this litter Miss S. Graham Weall bred some remarkable bitch puppies, who were later to prove their worth as outstanding broods, and dams of Champions. Among these were "Phidgity Phlare", "Phidgity Phlarepath of Philwil", "Phidgity Phlash's Girl". Unfortunately the lovely "Phidgity Phlash" died during her next whelping. Some of the most important results of these two noteworthy fawn and black matings will be described in the following chapter.

Though the gap in show activities caused by the Second World War was to cast its inevitable shadow, it did not succeed in quelling the enthusiasm of the small number of stalwarts who kept the Pug flag flying. In spite of feeding difficulties, the bravest managed to breed. Travelling was another handicap. More often than not matings took place with the nearest stud dog, rather than with the more carefully planned mate of one's choice. But they kept going, and all honour due to them.

Among the foremost must be mentioned Mr. G. W. Kerrod of 'Hopeworth' affix; Miss S. Graham Weall, 'Phidgity'; Mrs. Wendy Allen, 'Goldengleam'; Mrs. P. Williams. 'Philwil'; Miss M. Masland 'Masberk'; Mrs. Bancroft Wilson, 'Longlands'; the late Miss Gwen Atherton, 'Cedarwood'; and Miss E. H. McNair, 'Aynsley'.

4
Contemporary Dogs

A MEETING of the Pug Dog Club, the first since the end of the last war, was held in London in September, 1945. Our new secretary, who has remained with us ever since, was Mrs. S. F. Kearns. At a committee meeting later the same year, it was decided to hold our first post-war Club show. Eventually the date was settled for the first week in May, 1946, by which time the Kennel Club with post-war exuberance had decided on the hitherto unprecedented step of allocating Challenge Certificates to certain breed club shows. Miss M. D. Hatrick 'of Inver' was voted judge. The entry was 124 in the 18 classes, made by 43 individual exhibitors. To the blacks went the honour of winning both Challenge Certificates: Mr. Arthur Demaine's "Dark Dan", best dog and best of breed, and Mrs. Bancroft Wilson's "Blackberry of Longlands", best bitch. These two were brother and sister, and both soon won their titles: by "Dark Dando", out of "Dark Dinah", they were bred by the late Mrs. Clara Demaine, and were precursors in their line of the famous black Pugs who have graced the show ring since.

Unfortunately Ch. "Dark Dan" died early, soon after attaining his title, but his sister Ch. "Blackberry of Longlands" (or

'The Gremlin', as she was affectionately known), continued to distinguish herself as the great brood bitch she was. During her breeding time she produced five litters; her owner holding strong views against mixing the blacks with the fawns did her best to mate "Blackberry" to blacks only. She was mated to Miss M. Masland's "Hopeworth Chieftain", and to the same owner's "Tito of Masberk ", and it was to the latter dog she was most successful. Mated to him several times, she produced oustanding Pugs. Ch. "Blackberry" herself was well within the weight limit—she weighed 15 lb. One of her best daughters was "Lotus of Longlands", by "Tito of Masberk". She was purchased as a youngster by Mrs. Wyn Lewis. "Lotus" however waited to show her full prowess until she crossed the Atlantic. Mrs. Lewis accepted a tempting offer for her from the late Mr. Greenly of Pennsylvania, U.S.A., where she rapidly rose to the top, winning her American Championship. She also produced her first litter in the land of her adoption. To mention but a few other distinguished black winners from this strain, "Leslie of Longlands", "Black John of Longlands", litter brother to the American Champion "Lotus of Longlands" and "Black Girl of Longlands", who was purchased in 1947 by Lorna Countess Howe.

In Scotland, Miss Evelyn McNair, always a lover of the blacks, was busy with quite a number of good ones. In 1948 she still had "Linda of Lornesse", bred by Mrs. and Miss Betts, "Tansy of Aynsley", "Bluebell of Aynsley", and "Fairy of Aynsley", who were (starting with "Linda") great-grand-dam, grand-dam, dam and daughter, respectively.

Miss McNair has never ceased to further the cause of the breed. Though deeply attached to the blacks, she has been very successful with the fawns as well. Since the end of the war she has bred her first fawn Champion, Ch. "Geranium of Aynsley", by "Wolf of Aynsley" out of "Popette of Goldengleam". Miss McNair is also president of the Scottish Pug Dog Club.

Now to the famous fawn Pugs of this era. Mrs. Phyllis Williams ('Philwil') and her late husband Walter Williams, who was one of our most popular specialist judges, came very much to the fore. They had been far from idle during the war years, concentrating and breeding on the best lines, with the result that they presented the Pug world first of all with Ch. "Philwil Abbot" and his lovely litter sister Ch. "Philwil Amber". This brilliant pair fast made a name for the 'Philwil' kennel and their breeder.

The late Miss Gwen Atherton's Ch. Jacqueline of Cedarwood.

By "Chubby Chunks", owned by Mrs. E. Clugman, who later won his title and was by "Lucky Star of Cedarwood", out of "Phidgity Phlarepath of Philwil", out of "Philwil Bunty".

"Abbot" can safely claim to be one of the very best post-war Pugs. A gloriously boned dog, with large head, beautifully placed nose with width of muzzle, he was a true apricot fawn, standing at 17 1/2 lb. and winner of eight Challenge Certificates. He was a stud force of the highest order. Ch. "Philwil Amber" at 15 lb., darker in colour than her famous brother, was most beautiful for size, compact and symmetrical. "Abbot" was the male personified, whereas "Amber" was intensely feminine. She had the loveliest face with perfect nose placing, the darkest of dark eyes, 'like deep pools', and exquisite small button ears. Some preferred "Amber", others, the "Abbot": both had their share of admirers.

About this time I bought an eleven-months-old dog from the North. He was a great-grandson of my celebrated Ch. "Thunder-Cloud of Swainston", being out of "Phidgity Phlare" (already mentioned as coming from that litter containing those outstanding broods bred by Miss S. Graham Weall early in the war) and by the fawn "Wolf of Aynsley" bred by Miss McNair. He was Ch. "Silvio of Swainston", bred by Mrs. E. Bray. He was a small Pug for a male standing at 16 lb. in his prime. He was a very clear coloured fawn, with contrasting jet black points, and glorious head and wrinkle. He possessed the Peter Pan quality of eternal youth, and when he retired from the show ring at six years old, he

Ch. Thunder-Cloud of Swainston, owned by the author.

still looked no more than four years. The following is quoted from *Dog World,* 9th March, 1951:

> I think a small part of the history of Mrs. Swainston-Goodger's famous Pug, Ch. "Silvio of Swainston", might be an encouragement to others. This celebrated little dog won his first Challenge Certificate and Best of Breed at his first show. Not long after when on his way to another show, he had an accident which resulted in the slipping of the stifle joint in his hind leg. He was lame for a long time, hope was given up, and it appeared as if his show days were over, but everything possible was done. At last he gradually became less lame, until the limb was sound again. Radiography revealed the joint to have completely righted itself. He returned to the ring to win his second Challenge Certificate and Best of Breed at Richmond in 1948. Since then he has won eight more Challenge Certificates, and has been six times Best of Breed—won ten Challenge Certificates in all, which was a post-war record for his breed, during his lifetime. It only goes to prove

that when things are at their worst, there is always a chance of avoiding disaster.

Mention here again must be made of "Phidgity Phlare". Besides being dam of Ch. "Silvio of Swainston", she was dam of Mrs. Crawford's fawn dog Ch. "Fordcraw Beauty", by "Coral of Aynsley."

Ch. "Philwil Candy" bred the same way as Ch. "Chubby Chunks" was mated to Ch. "Silvio of Swainston", and produced Ch. "Phidgity Phyllis", bred by Mrs. P. Williams. Another daughter of Ch. "Silvio" to become a Champion was Ch. "Phidgity Marquita of Petrozanne", out of "Antoinette of Chetrose", bred by Mrs. Carmen Roberts and owned by Miss S. Graham Weall. Ch. "Phidgity Phyllis", who became, and has always remained, the property of Miss S. Graham Weall, was a lovely bitch. She was a clear fawn with plentiful wrinkle, lovely head, twist and bone, a glorious body and constructed both for show and breeding, which is the ideal for a bitch, I think. She was mated several times to Ch. "Philwil Abbot". This was indeed a union which made history —presenting the Pug world with no less than four Champions: Ch. "Phidgity Phyl's Son", Ch. "Phidgity Philbert" (owned and jockeyed to fame by Mrs. M. B. Kendrick, who was

Miss S. Graham Weall's Ch. Phidgity Phyllis.

also the breeder and owner of his son, Ch. "Markendon Bengy") and Chs. "Ducray Phidgity Phyllida" and "Phenella". The 'Ducray' kennels, owned by Mrs. Wyn Lewis, also made up Ch. "Hopeworth Prima Donna" bred by Mr. G. W. Kerrod, and Ch. "Philwil Josephine" bred by Mrs P. Williams, who was by Ch. "Philwil Abbot" out of Ch. "Philwil Candy". Mrs. Wyn Lewis bred Ch. "Ducray Daniel", sold as a puppy to Major Rushton, who made him up—he was by "Justso of Cedarwood" out of Ch. "Ducray Phidgity Phyllida", and Ch. "Ducray Amanda" by Ch. "Phidgity Philbert" out of Ch. "Philwil Josephine". Ch. "Ducray Amanda" later became the property of Miss S. Graham Weall. Most of Mrs. Lewis's best Pugs were fawn.

Mrs. Wendy Allen of 'Goldengleam' affix has bred many good Pugs. Some of her best went overseas or on the Continent, becoming Champions in the lands of their adoption. The fawn "Goldengleam Trooper", who was shown at Cruft's in 1953, went abroad to join the Duke and Duchess of Windsor and their other Canadian-bred Pug "Disraele". Mrs. Allen's famous fawns were descended from "Peach Cloud of Swainston", daughter of Ch. "Thunder-Cloud of Swainston", who was mated to her fawn dog "Prince Raleigh of St. Elmo". This union produced two notable Pugs—"Cobby John of Goldengleam", who remained in the ownership of his breeder, and his litter sister "Dutch Girl of Goldengleam", who became the property of the late Mr. and Mrs. Harold Heap.

Miss W. M. Steggall's Ch. Capers of Swainston, exported to Canada in 1938.

Mr. and Mrs. Heap held the special distinction of bravely keeping the Pug flag flying by showing at every opportunity in variety classes at the few small shows which took place during the wartime. "Dutch Girl", though already five years old when the Championship shows restarted after the war, managed to win her first two Challenge Certificates. It was only a combination of bad luck and Anno Domini which prevented her winning her title, which otherwise she would have richly deserved.

In 1943 Mrs. Allen purchased a black bitch puppy from Mr. Kerrod, "Hopeworth San Toy", by the black "Hopeworth Democrat", out of the fawn "Hopeworth Sunflower". This was her first black Pug, part of the foundation of some of the best black postwar Pugs we have had. Soon after the end of the war Mrs. Allen's kennels were struck by a bad visitation of distemper, but undaunted this intrepid breeder carried on. Her own greatest distinction was the home-bred black bitch Ch. "Goldengleam Shotsilk" by "Black John of Longlands" out of "Goldengleam Inkspot". "Black John", of course, was bred by Mrs. Bancroft Wilson, and as before mentioned, was litter brother to the American Ch. "Lotus of Longlands."

Mrs. Phyllis Williams continued to be highly successful in the show ring. Many tip top quality Pugs of her breeding made their mark both at home and abroad. Her "Philwil Cherub", by Ch. "Philwil Abbot" out of Ch. "Philwil Candy", was sold to Miss Nellie Wakefield, in whose hands he won his title and became Ch. "Philwil Cherub of Glenva". He was later sold to Messrs. Stewart and Clinton Allen of Maryville, Kansas City. The latest 'Philwil' Champion in this country is Ch. "Philwil Hermit" by "Kunetown Kadet of Philwil", out of Ch. "Philwil Amber."

From Northumberland hails Mrs. Irena Walker of 'Tynestad' prefix. Her first to attain the heights was the fawn Ch. "Tynestad Erna" by Ch. "Fordcraw Beauty", out of "Sandra of Greengables". She was bred by the well-known Northern breeder Miss Dorothy Forster. During 1956 Mrs. Walker's fawn dog Ch. "Tynestad Singaria" won his title. He is by "Philwil Cloister", out of Ch. "Tynestad Erna."

From the Midlands Miss Dorothy Wildgoose of 'Pugholme' affix came to the fore with her black bitch Ch. "Bunty of Pugholme", and her fawn kennel mate Ch. "Pugholme Catherine of Harloo". Her latest to make the grade is the home-bred fawn dog Ch. "Tinker of Pugholme."

Mrs. Phyllis Williams' Ch. Philwil Abbot.

Mr. J. H. and Miss N. Wakefield 'of Glenva' affix brought forward their second fawn Champion, the home-bred Ch. "Glenbrumas of Glenva" by Ch. "Bluedoor Puggypug Titus", out of "Glenpenny of Glenva."

Further distinguished specimens of this era which deserve recording are Ch. "Bricett", a fawn dog bred by Mr. W. Elliott, by "Phil of Myondo" out of "Damsel Divine", was owned by, and gained his title with, the Rev. L. H. Cumberland, and has since become the property of Miss M. Masland; Ch. "Philip of Modelhouse" bred by Mrs. E. Dore, by "Jumbo of Modelhouse" out of "Gwnnet of Modelhouse", and sold as a puppy to Mrs. Douglas Bunn; Ch. "Nova Horace", owned and bred by Mrs. U. Porritt, by Ch. "Philwil Abbot" out of "Grenewyn Jenny Wren"; Ch. "It's It of Cedarwood", bred by the late Miss Atherton, and owned by Mrs. S. H. Clough, by "Tom Thumb of Le Tasyll" out of "It's Me of Cedarwood"; and Ch. "Marigold of Evertrue", bred by Mrs. Hunt Lewis, also by her "Tom Thumb of Le Tasyll" out of "Annabelle of Cedarwood". She was owned by Mrs. A. M. Elcome, in whose hands she attained her title. She finally became the property of Miss Atherton.

Mrs. D. M. Connors of 'Bluedoor' prefix exported the black dog Ch. "Bluedoor Puggypug Titus" in 1953 to America. He was sold to the late Mr. Greenly who had already imported "Lotus of Longlands". He was by Mrs. Connors' fawn dog "Masberk Automne" and out of the black "Lily of Longlands", and was bred by Mrs. G. Featherstone of 'Puggypug' prefix. He was the third of our best dogs to go overseas. In 1938 I sold a black puppy to Miss W. M. Steggall, 'Winna' prefix of Canada, who later became Int. Ch. "Capers of Swainston". This dog, besides siring the black Int. Ch. "Winna Canadian Capers", sired the fawn Int. Ch. "Winna John Peel". "Capers" was bred the same way as our celebrated Ch. "Thunder-Cloud of Swainston". This black dog had a powerful influence in Canada and America, where numerous of his Champion progeny found their way. The second valuable stud force export, already mentioned, was the fawn Ch. "Philwil Cherub of Glenva."

About this period those falling under the spell of the Pug increased in numbers. In the show world many enthusiasts in other breeds took on Pugs as an extra line.

Noteworthy amongst these has been Lady Howe of celebrated 'Banchory' prefix, and Mrs. W. S. Young 'of Rydens'. Both these ladies came from bigger dogs to fall for the charm of the Pug. In 1947 Lady Howe in partnership with her companion Miss Lang purchased her first black Pug, bred by Mrs. Bancroft Wilson, "Banchory Black Girl of Longlands". She had already got a fawn, "Banchory Robena of Grenewyn", bred by Mr. Arthur Green of Wakefield. "Black Girl" won best puppy at the Pug Club Show, May, 1947, before she went to Lady Howe, and soon afterwards she joined her companion "Robena". These two have remained special house pets ever since.

It has taken Lady Howe only a very few years to achieve remarkable success in the show ring with Pugs. Up to date blacks have been her strong line. She made her first Champion in 1954 with Ch. "Banchory Bluedoor Taffeta", bred by Mrs. P. M. Connors, by the aforementioned exported black dog Ch. "Bluedoor Puggypug Titus", out of "Banchory Bluedoor Tessa", also bred by Mrs. Connors. Her next was the homebred Ch. "Banchory Silk", by Ch. "Archibald of Rydens" out of "Banchory Goldengleam Velvet Coon". Unfortunately "Silk" died with none of her only litter surviving her. So far the star is Ch. "Banchory Lace", a

Ch. Banchory Lace, bred and owned by Lorna Countess Howe and Miss Lang.

younger sister of the late Ch. "Banchory Silk". This beautiful little bitch has now won twenty-two Challenge Certificates, thirty-three Best of Breed, and fourteen Best in Show awards. No less than three choice black males of Mrs. Wendy Allen's breeding were purchased by this kennel, as well as "Banchory Goldengleam Velvet Coon", dam of the first home-bred 'Banchory' Champions.

Mrs. W. S. Young 'of Rydens' affix has also been successful in a remarkably short time. In 1951 she bred the black dog who became Ch. "Archibald of Rydens", by Ch. "Bluedoor Puggypug Titus" out of her black "Mimi of Elmsleigh", bred by Mrs. Gibson. 'Born to be a Champion' might well have been this dog's password. He had nearly all, and seemingly enough, to achieve his great successes, both as show dog and stud force, not the least of his attributes being a marvellous show temperament, of which full advantage was taken by his skilful owner. Her second Pug Champion, a black dog, is Ch. "Kandy of Rydens", a grandson of Ch. "Archibald of Rydens".

Other well-known exhibitors who have come into Pugs from other breeds are Mr. Joslin of 'St. Olam' prefix and St. Bernards' fame, and Miss Varley, who have already made three Champions, namely, the late Ch. "St. Olam Bingo", Ch. "St. Olam Chubby", and Ch. "St. Olam Shindy"; also Mrs. Coventon and her daughter Miss Butt of 'Adastra' prefix and world-wide Poodle reputation, who own the black dog Ch. "Adastra Goldengleam Bouncer's Boy", another bred by Mrs. Wendy Allen. He is by "Jester of Le Tasyll", out of Ch. "Goldengleam Shotsilk".

Mrs. A. Cotes owns Ch. "Corbury Sammy of Goldengleam", yet another distinguished black bred by Mrs. Wendy Allen. He is by Ch. "Archibald of Rydens", out of "Goldengleam Pansy Face."

Ch. "Hazelbridge Paul", bred by Mrs. Amice Pitt of Cavalier King Charles Spaniel fame, and owned by Mrs. M. Cuming of French Bulldog fame, is a beautiful very clear fawn, just the right size. He is by the late Ch. "Phidgity Philbert", ex "Sugar Plum of Ttiweh".

5

Formation of the Pug Dog Club

 E have three Pug Dog clubs in Great Britain. The leader, or mother club, as we may call it, is the original Pug Dog Club first formed in the year 1883. The other two are the Scottish Pug Dog Club and the Northern Pug Dog Club.

The idea of a Pug Dog Club in England was discussed in correspondence appearing in the *Stockkeeper* in 1881. Among other things, it was suggested that the well-known canine writer and judge Hugh Dalziel be invited to become a foundation member of the proposed club. Dalziel himself wrote to the *Stockkeeper* in the same year, approving the idea of a Pug club, but reminding Pug enthusiasts that the foundation of an official club often led to 'cliques' or bad feeling among dog breeders—I leave readers to decide for themselves whether this warning may not ring as true today!

The fact that Dalziel took part in this correspondence is interesting since the Standard eventually adopted by the Pug Dog Club was based on his writings in his *British Dogs,* which first appeared in 1880. The Pug Dog Club was finally formed in 1883, and a full report of the inaugural meeting can be found in the

March issue of the *Kennel Gazette* of that year. One object of that meeting was to settle the Standard of the breed, which is set out in the report. It is a shortened version adopted without acknowledgement of Dalziel's opinion on the points of the Pug printed in his *British Dogs*. Several of the phrases, e.g. 'multum in parvo', 'the eyes . . . very lustrous, and when excited, full of fire' are taken word for word from Dalziel.

In his *Prize Dogs of America and England* (1891) Dr. Cryer wrote that judges in America at that time applied either one of the two Standards, the Standard set out by 'Stonehenge' (J. H. Walsh) in his *The Dogs of the British Islands,* 1867, or the Standard arranged and issued by the English Pug Dog Club.

At any rate what we may call the Dalziel Standard superseded the 'Stonehenge' Standard and became the official Pug Standard recognized by the Kennel Club. It has stood the test of time, and remains unchanged to the present day, except that the recommended weight of the Pug given in the original Standard as from 13 to 17 lb. (dog or bitch) was altered some time before the Second World War to, as from 15 lb. and later 14 to 18 lb. with the addition of the qualifying adjective 'desirable.'

It is of interest to note that the Scottish Pug Dog Club, which issued its set of show points in 1925, likewise derived from Dalziel, stuck to the original weight 13 to 17 lb. (dog or bitch) until 1949, when the Scottish members conformed to the same weight Standard as the Pug Dog Club. The Northern Pug Dog Club had always adopted the same Standard as the Pug Dog Club, so now all three clubs in Great Britain follow the same Standard originated by Hugh Dalziel over seventy years ago.

6

The Standard

General Appearance—A decidedly square and cobby dog. The Pug should be 'multum in parvo', but this condensation should be shown by compactness of form, well knit proportions, and hardness of developed muscle.

Head and Skull—Head large, massive, round—not apple-headed, with no indentation of the skull. Muzzle short, blunt, square but not up-faced. Wrinkles large and deep.

Eyes—Dark in colour, very large, bold and prominent, globular in shape, soft and solicitous in expression, very lustrous and when excited full of fire.

Ears—Thin, small, soft, like black velvet. There are two kinds—the 'rose' and the 'button'. Preference should be given to the latter.

Forequarters—Legs very strong, straight, of moderate length, and well under the body.

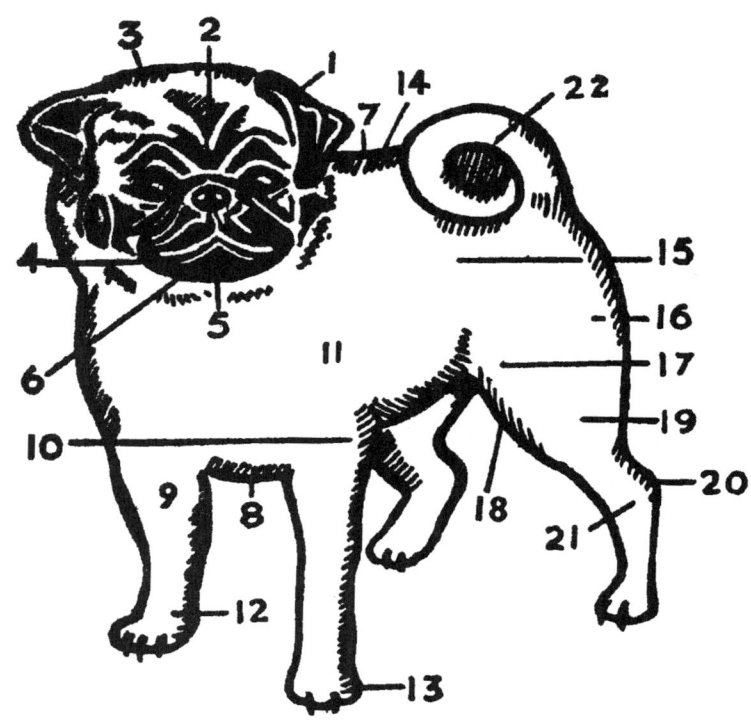

DIAGRAM OF THE POINTS OF A PUG

1. Ear
2. Nose and Stop
3. Skull
4. Lips
5. Underjaw
6. Throat
7. Withers
8. Brisket
9. Arm
10. Point of Elbow
11. Shoulder
12. Wrist
13. Toes
14. Back
15. Loin
16. Buttock
17. Flank
18. Stifle Joint
19. Thigh
20. Point of Hock
21. Hock
22. Twist

Body—Short and cobby, wide in chest and well ribbed.

Hindquarters—Legs very strong, straight, of moderate length, and well under.

Feet—Neither so long as the foot of the hare, nor so round as that of the cat; well split-up toes; the nails black.

(Tail Twist)—Curled tightly as possible over the hips. The double curl is perfection.

Coat—Fine, smooth, soft, short and glossy, neither hard nor woolly.

Colour—Silver, apricot fawn or black. Each should be clearly decided, to make the contrast complete between the colour, the trace and the mark. Markings: clearly defined. The muzzle or mask, ears, marks on cheeks, thumb-mark or diamond on forehead and the trace should be as black as possible. Mask: the mask should be black, the more intense and well defined, the better. Trace: a black line extending from the occiput to the twist.

Weight and Size—Desirable weight from 14 to 18 lb. (dog or bitch).

Faults—Lean, leggy. Short legs and long body.

POINTS

	Fawn Points	*Black Points*
Symmetry	10	10
Size	5	10
Condition	5	5
Body	10	10
Legs	5	5

POINTS — continued

	Fawn Points	*Black Points*
Feet	—	—
Head	5	5
Muzzle	10	10
Ears	5	5
Eyes	10	10
Mark	5	—
Wrinkles	5	5
Tail	10	10
Trace	5	—
Coat	5	5
Colour	5	10

The best Standard for any breed is that which sets down as clearly and simply as possible the desirable attributes to be attained so that breeders have a sound aim in view and judges may accordingly take note. If we are all striving towards the same ideal not only should we recognize our own and others' successes when we see them, but our breed will have a solid basis of achievement to be enhanced by each future generation of breeders.

The Standard is designed as a guide to the newcomer, as well as a permanent reminder for all concerned with the breed. It cannot be a lengthy epistle and whilst including what is most important,

The author's Ch. Mandor Susie and Ch. Prempeh of Hopeworth.

it must be free from irrelevancies. Nevertheless its compilation should embody a lifelike effect. If dull, it will not provide the desirable picture for all to emulate. As Standards go, I think that that of the Pug Dog Club is very good. Generations of Pug breeders have bred, exhibited and passed on, but our Standard has never needed to be radically amended, and has stood the test of time. So let us pay a just tribute, though a belated one, to the memory of that wise man Hugh Dalziel whom we have to thank for our good, sound Standard today.

Ch. Ducray Amanda, bred and owned by Mrs. Wyn Lewis.

I would like to make some comments on the classification of the breed as a Toy dog, and on the subject of weight with its bearing on size.

As everyone knows, the Pug Dog is rightly classified as a Toy dog, and this important point has always been taken for granted in the description in the Standard on General Appearance.

Now about weight in relation to size. Many newcomers to the Pug cult have been puzzled at seeing Pugs of different sizes showing together, small, medium and large, and have questioned—'What is the right size then?' In former days when there seemed more time for everything, the weighing machine was sometimes resorted to, and, if not wholly satisfactory, it helped to throw some light on the problem, as, if the exhibit weighed over or under the Standard weight, he was considered too large or too small. Since those times, the weight has been altered more than once, and the qualification of 'desirable' added, it must be admitted somewhat in favour of the larger Pugs, the question being left to the individual judge's decision. Some think this is wrong, and that a stricter adherence to the letter of the Standard should be insisted upon. They say the Pug as a Toy dog should be of smaller or medium size so as to conform more to the set down Standard. Others do not at all object to the larger size, and in the absence of proof by weighing, they are content to profit by the elasticity of the term 'desirable' so that handsome Pugs of up to 20 lb. and over have got away without being penalised.

Ch. Adastra Goldengleam Bouncer's Boy, owned by Mrs. Coventon and Miss Butt.

No doubt most of us have our favourite size. I myself, for instance, prefer a Pug of smaller to medium size conforming as nearly as possible with the Standard. An experienced judge will know how to spot his 'multum in parvo', together with the other requirements set out in 'General Appearance' of the Standard, and a Pug conforming to this, may rightly appeal to the experienced eye as a 'lovely size.'

Other factors influencing size, I believe to be fashion and feeding. Towards the end of the last century, and in the earlier years of this one, we know that some Pugs were very much smaller. This was the time when the Pug Dog Club adopted the weight Standard of from 13 lb. to 17 lb. If there had been a qualifying 'desirable' then, it would assuredly have favoured the smaller Pugs. It is clear from this, and other evidence from early photographs and prints that small Pugs were fashionable in those days of long ago. Fashion and convention play their parts in influencing the trend in size.

In those days Toy dogs were considered ladies' dogs, and they were usually called lap-dogs, which calls to mind that ladies really had laps then for their little dogs to sit in. They had both the time and the means. The fashion in ladies' dress was, of course, extremely different: voluminous dresses, not to mention petticoats, all that was needed in fact to create a comfortable lap for her little dog, who had to follow the fashion to hold his place as my lady's favourite, by keeping himself small. Small enough for her to bend her corseted figure easily, pick him up and carry him

Miss S. Graham Weall's Phidgity Phlash and Phidgity Paprika.

about with her. How different nowadays! Pug's mistress no longer has the time to spare to sit and nurse him in her lap. Her dress is rightly designed for free and speedy movement, and gone is the full drapery which was the foundation of Pug's lap before. Gone also perhaps is the need for the Pug to be so small, and so the fashion gradually changes until we get used to seeing larger present-day Pugs often competing successfully at the shows.

Feeding too in those earlier days was different. It was generally accepted that meat made dogs fierce, gave them worms and made the breath smell. If he wasn't robbed of his vital proteins in the form of meat, he might by contrast be grossly overfed. Now-a-days we know dog feeding, particularly of show dogs and breeding stock, is almost a science, and no self respecting

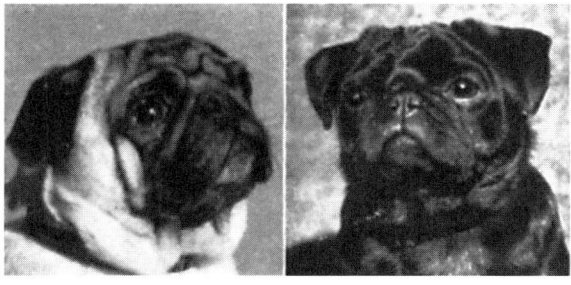

Mrs. B. H. Grimshaw's His Honour of Swainston and Mrs. V. Graham's homebred Ch. Edenderry Cuan.

dog allows himself to be done out of his regular meat supply. Thus a good and plentiful diet may well play its part in the production of some of the larger Pugs, just as improved nutrition has been statistically proved to increase size in children.

All the same, a warning note should be given on not allowing the Pug to become too large. From time to time a judge raises his voice in protest, as at a recent Toy dog show, the judge's critique read:

> Size is another point that wants watching. If this is not kept in check it will be farcical to continue to call some breeds Toys. I would particularly apply this to Black-and-Tan Terriers, Cavaliers and Pugs.

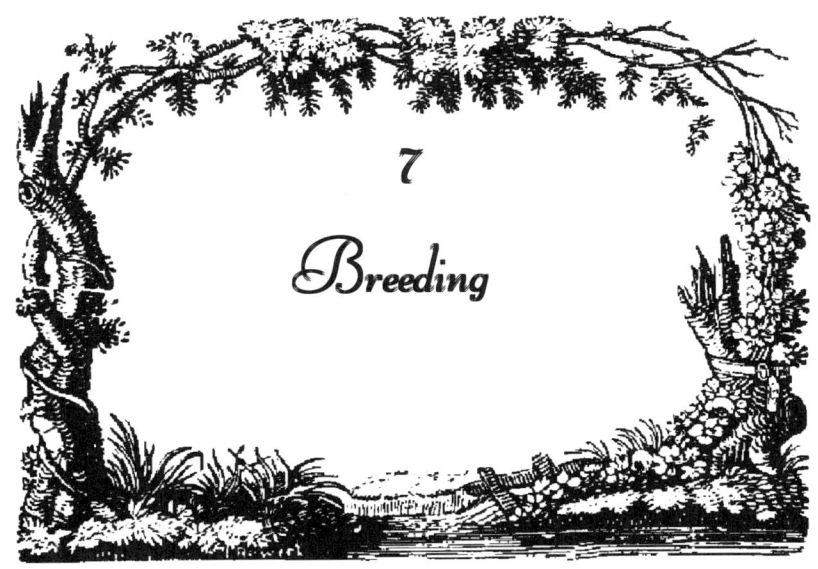

7
Breeding

ANY distinguished breeders have found their vocation by starting as pet owners, almost by chance—'I didn't really intend to have a Pug, but now we have become so fond of him, I can't imagine having any other breed'.

This is where the pet owner stops, and certainly his destiny may be an easier one than that of the person who decides to go further, for whom the next best thing to do, is to find out as much as possible about the breed.

Delve into the various dog books, old and new. Gaze upon pictures of Pugs, and above all, study and re-study the Standard. Check up your own Pug and any others you may see with the Standard. Then make a point of attending shows where there are Pug classes. All the leading dog shows are advertised in the dog papers *Dog World* and *Our Dogs*. One is liable to be confused at one's first shows and it is not surprising to feel somewhat bewildered. Watch, listen and learn as much as you can, study the show catalogues to make yourself familiar with the different breeders, dogs and names. If you can afford not to be in too much of a hurry before planning your campaign for a start, so much the better.

By now you should have a pretty good idea whether your existing Pug, if you have one, is worth breeding from. If a bitch, you will have to decide on a suitable mate for her. If a dog, you may consider the purchase of a suitable bitch for him, with the view of starting your breeding venture in earnest. Should you, however, want to buy your first Pugs for breeding, all that has been said equally applies, and in this case your best plan would be to buy one or two well-bred young bitches, as unrelated as possible. A young bitch about six months or under a year old would be a good age, or even one a little older who has had her first season as you would not consider mating her until her second season.

The difficulty here is that young bitches of this age, if good enough, might be harder to obtain, even at fancy prices. You may have Beginner's Luck, which has happened before. However, if such a delectable young 'lady' was offered to you, have due caution before buying to obtain satisfactory reasons as to why the breeder or owner is willing to part with her.

It might be easier to buy a nice bitch puppy at about eight weeks old. You could rear her yourself and have the pleasure of her puppyhood, which would be an experience in itself. You would have ample time to look around, take or discard different advice given you about a suitable dog to have her mated to at her second coming into season. Do not fix on a stud dog chiefly because he happens to be a Champion, unless he also happens to be the very dog you would have chosen for your bitch, apart from his title. You may be persuaded that puppies by a Champion will sell easily and at better prices. In most cases the Champion stud dogs are so constantly used, that there are likely to be several litters by them at the same time as yours arrives. It is a pity some breeders flock like sheep after certain Champions, as it is not good for the breed to flood the market with increasing supplies of ever more closely related puppies.

One could go on for ever trying to describe the right way, and giving warning of the pitfalls. The truth is, there is no short cut to ultimate success. Time and experience alone must be lived through if you are to succeed, and this does not only mean winning prizes at shows, but leaving on your breed the stamp of having served it well.

There has been an increasing boom in Pugs since the end of the last war, due to many new people taking up the breed. Whether this will last re-

Ch. Goldengleam Shotsilk, bred and owned by Mrs. Wendy Allen.

mains to be seen. There have been periods in the past when Pugs had great booms too. Warning must be given against inbreeding, and reckless attempts, such as continually using the same line because it has produced a particular show winning type.

Within the last decade before the war, breeders of that day had brought the breed to a better state of affairs in this respect than now exists. At least half-a-dozen different strains, and each recognizable by distinct individual type, were available. This made for a sound breeding proposition. The present now prevalent custom of restriction to type by using the same stud dogs is a short-sighted policy, particularly for the future. It is not an easy problem. The great antiquity of the breed has a bearing on its smaller population, as well as the inevitable relativity of its members: another reason for thoughtful selection by breeders.

In other breeds of dogs, such as the Boxer, the situation can be improved upon by importing fresh stock if required from abroad. Any hope of obtaining Pugs from the original source, i.e. China, can practically be eliminated since during the last thirty or so years selective breeding of the old Chinese breeds such as the Pug and Pekingese has languished, and under the present regime can hardly be said to exist at all. As for other contemporary

European Pugs, we can save the anxieties of quarantine by discovering that importation of outside Pug blood is hardly worth the outlay. A few years ago a young fawn Pug was imported from the Continent not even collaterally related to any of our existing British lines. This would indeed have been of inestimable value had one been able to use him to introduce a purely fresh blood line, but alas! he was such an out and out non-conformist to our Standard, that he was never used for stud, and became a beloved pet instead. And Pugs from America, Canada and Australia are too much bred to our own already exported stock to be of much use to us as fresh blood

MATING

Pugs as a breed have distinct idiosyncrasies of their own, which it is well to be prepared for. Usually they choose to take their time over their affairs, notably at mating and during whelping, though no hard and fast rule can be laid down. The courting couple like to take their time. The Pug is not one to be hustled or hurried, and the same can be said of the whelping bitch in most cases. It is not a good plan to be in too much of a hurry to start a

Ch. Tinker of Pugholm, bred and owned by Miss D. Wildgoose.

young dog at stud. He should not be put to his first bitch before he is twelve months old, at which age, if he seems well and fit, he can be used for the first time preferably to a bitch who is a proved brood. Thereafter he should not have another bitch until he is fourteen months old. After this he may be considered to have qualified for his profession, and he can be put at regular stud.

Though here we are chiefly considering the bitch owner, I would say if you happen to have a good young dog, and want to use him at stud, it is as well to train him from his first time, for his career. This only consists in organizing a state of control over the proceedings, and whilst too much interference is not recommended, it is almost as bad to let a stud run wild, which means his having his own way all the time. Some novices start off with the innocent illusion that so long as the bitch is in season, one only has to dump the couple down together, and Nature will do the rest.

Like 'Love at First Sight' sometimes it comes off, but it is the exception rather than the rule. Of the two, the dog being the active member, his role is more important. It is quite surprising how many small matters there are, any one of which can put a stud dog off his job, resulting in failure and disappointment all round. This is where that little bit of training comes in. If a young dog is allowed to tire himself by getting over-excited before the mating takes place, or equally so through the bitch being fractious or difficult, he may of a sudden make up his mind he is fed up, and won't try any more. Once a Pug starts getting obstinate, one might as well give up. This is why it is very worthwhile to get your dog used to you handling the bitch as you often have to, to keep her steady for him, and also not to object to any judicious handling of himself, if necessary. The value of this lies in the less likelihood of your dog developing into what is known as a moody stud: an unreliable worker who sometimes will and sometimes won't. Apart from disappointing the bitch owner, he loses the fee he might have earned, and above all, you can also ill afford risking loss to his reputation—'I took her to Ch. "Tom Tom", but he just wouldn't mate her!'

The bitch comes into season twice a year, at an interval of six months, her first about the time of puberty, which is normally between eight and twelve months old, though Pugs can be variable in their times, some bitches coming in season earlier, and others have been known to miss the second season altogether, and only come into 'use' as it is called once a year. Note should be made of the day your bitch first 'shows colour', as this is the day from which you count, as she is generally ready for mating at about her twelfth day.

If it is the second season, and you have already booked the stud dog for her, inform the owner as soon as your bitch comes into season, so that there will be ample time to make arrangements for her journey and reception. The stud dog owner will tell you what day the bitch is to be taken, or sent by rail or road in a closed hamper. The latter method, besides being less costly, is usually the best, providing, of course, you have full confidence in the people to whom she is going. It is probable that the dog's owner will suggest her arriving a day or two before her twelfth day, so that she may get time to settle down in her new surroundings, before the day she is to be mated.

In general, should the bitch's owner insist on accompanying her, it may make her inclined to cling to owner and home memories to such a degree as to cause her at the best to be more fractious and difficult than she would have been by herself, or at the worst, make her such a 'silly girl' as to develop a determination against being mated at all, and if necessary to fight for all she is worth at any attempt to separate her from her owner. This in its turn may easily put off the stud altogether, particularly if he is a sensitive dog. There is always the exception to the rule, e.g. the bitch

Mrs. S. Bancroft Wilson's Ch. Blackberry of Longlands, from the painting by M. A. Edmonds.

who might be inspired with confidence by the presence of her owner throughout. On the other hand, this could shift the trouble to the other side, as the stud dog usually resents the presence of a stranger. If you must accompany your bitch you are well advised, having satisfied yourself that the dog of your choice is to be used, to absent yourself during the mating. You can always request to be summoned when the pair are 'tied' or 'locked' should you want the evidence of your own eyes that the mating has taken place.

WHELPING

The period of gestation counted from the day of mating is sixty-three days, but Pugs frequently whelp a day or two sooner than the sixty-third. It is best to have all ready for the whelping well in advance. Pugs seldom carry their young beyond the sixty-third day. It is always well to have your veterinary surgeon acquainted with the bitch beforehand, and notified of the date of her expected whelping, then, should his help be required, he can be summoned quickly.

Pugs are very good mothers; as a rule they should whelp as easily as any of the other small dogs, but they are not expected to be self whelpers, and you must be prepared to be in attendance. If this is your first experience, you may have arranged to have your vet for the event. In any case you should be prepared for possible emergencies. Your bitch may start to whelp in the middle of the night, or in the early hours of the morning. If you can get an experienced doggy friend to come along and help you, so much the better. You would have the opportunity of observation, and learn quite a lot of what has to be done, so that for another time you would have gained sufficient confidence to cope with a normal whelping yourself.

The whole dimension of the subject cannot adequately be described in a manual of this size. An attempt only can be made to give some of the principal aspects to expect, together with a list of a few of the necessary articles to have in readiness, as follows:

> Small pair of surgical scissors.
> Small basin with warm water and Dettol for whelping attendant's hand washing.
> Bowl with Dettol and water to keep scissors in when they are not in use.
> Hand towel for attendant.
> Piece of old, soft Turkish towelling to grip and help puppy with on way out, if necessary.
> Small saucepan for warming up bitch's occasional milk tipple.
> Kettle.
> Covered hot-water bottle for temporary puppy box.
> Slop pail for afterbirths, etc.
> Plenty of newspapers, and hot and cold water.

Heating arrangements depend on the time of the year. Warmth is the rule, and extra warmth is necessary in the winter time. Though oppressive heat is never advisable, heating must be readily available, and there must be means on the spot of boiling the kettle, and warming up the bitch's small milk drinks which she may gratefully lap up, after each delivery.

The bitch should whelp in her own roomy whelping box which has been previously settled upon. Underneath and surrounding it several thicknesses of newspaper can be spread out. Another smaller box should be in readiness, preferably out of the bitch's line of vision, in case she perversely tries to occupy it herself, in preference to her own lying-in box. This extra box is useful to place each newly arrived puppy in, as soon as the bitch shows signs that she is getting busy with another arrival. The puppies' box should have comfortable bedding in it, a hot-water bottle covered with flannel, and a blanket over the hot-water bottle folded double, bag-wise, inside which the puppy or puppies can be placed. A small shawl can be tucked in over the blanket, as the little creatures must be kept warm.

TABLE SHOWING WHEN A BITCH IS DUE TO WHELP

Served Jan.	Whelps March	Served Feb.	Whelps April	Served March	Whelps May	Served April	Whelps June	Served May	Whelps July	Served June	Whelps Aug	Served July	Whelps Sept	Served Aug	Whelps Oct	Served Sept	Whelps Nov.	Served Oct	Whelps Dec.	Served Nov	Whelps Jan.	Served Dec.	Whelps Feb.
1	5	1	5	1	3	1	3	1	3	1	3	1	2	1	3	1	3	1	3	1	3	1	2
2	6	2	6	2	4	2	4	2	4	2	4	2	3	2	4	2	4	2	4	2	4	2	3
3	7	3	7	3	5	3	5	3	5	3	5	3	4	3	5	3	5	3	5	3	5	3	4
4	8	4	8	4	6	4	6	4	6	4	6	4	5	4	6	4	6	4	6	4	6	4	5
5	9	5	9	5	7	5	7	5	7	5	7	5	6	5	7	5	7	5	7	5	7	5	6
6	10	6	10	6	8	6	8	6	8	6	8	6	7	6	8	6	8	6	8	6	8	6	7
7	11	7	11	7	9	7	9	7	9	7	9	7	8	7	9	7	9	7	9	7	9	7	8
8	12	8	12	8	10	8	10	8	10	8	10	8	9	8	10	8	10	8	10	8	10	8	9
9	13	9	13	9	11	9	11	9	11	9	11	9	10	9	11	9	11	9	11	9	11	9	10
10	14	10	14	10	12	10	12	10	12	10	12	10	11	10	12	10	12	10	12	10	12	10	11
11	15	11	15	11	13	11	13	11	13	11	13	11	12	11	13	11	13	11	13	11	13	11	12
12	16	12	16	12	14	12	14	12	14	12	14	12	13	12	14	12	14	12	14	12	14	12	13
13	17	13	17	13	15	13	15	13	15	13	15	13	14	13	15	13	15	13	15	13	15	13	14
14	18	14	18	14	16	14	16	14	16	14	16	14	15	14	16	14	16	14	16	14	16	14	15
15	19	15	19	15	17	15	17	15	17	15	17	15	16	15	17	15	17	15	17	15	17	15	16
16	20	16	20	16	18	16	18	16	18	16	18	16	17	16	18	16	18	16	18	16	18	16	17
17	21	17	21	17	19	17	19	17	19	17	19	17	18	17	19	17	19	17	19	17	19	17	18
18	22	18	22	18	20	18	20	18	20	18	20	18	19	18	20	18	20	18	20	18	20	18	19
19	23	19	23	19	21	19	21	19	21	19	21	19	20	19	21	19	21	19	21	19	21	19	20
20	24	20	24	20	22	20	22	20	22	20	22	20	21	20	22	20	22	20	22	20	22	20	21
21	25	21	25	21	23	21	23	21	23	21	23	21	22	21	23	21	23	21	23	21	23	21	22
22	26	22	26	22	24	22	24	22	24	22	24	22	23	22	24	22	24	22	24	22	24	22	23
23	27	23	27	23	25	23	25	23	25	23	25	23	24	23	25	23	25	23	25	23	25	23	24
24	28	24	28	24	26	24	26	24	26	24	26	24	25	24	26	24	26	24	26	24	26	24	25
25	29	25	29	25	27	25	27	25	27	25	27	25	26	25	27	25	27	25	27	25	27	25	26
26	30	26	30	26	28	26	28	26	28	26	28	26	27	26	28	26	28	26	28	26	28	26	27
27	31	27	1	27	29	27	29	27	29	27	29	27	28	27	29	27	29	27	29	27	29	27	28
28	1	28	2	28	30	28	30	28	30	28	30	28	29	28	30	28	30	28	30	28	30	28	1
29	2	29	3	29	31	29	1	29	31	29	31	29	30	29	31	29	1	29	31	29	31	29	2
30	3			30	1	30	2	30	1	30	1	30	1	30	1	30	2	30	1	30	1	30	3
31	4			31	2			31	2			31	2	31	2			31	2			31	4

As soon as the bitch has settled down again, after the delivery of a newcomer, and has licked him well, we hope, and had her milk tipple, the rest of the family can all be quickly and gently put back to her in the whelping box, as the sooner they all get sucking the better, though special attention should be given to the latest arrival in this respect, as being the least experienced member of the family up to date.

Usually the bitch will show signs of her approaching travail sometime in advance. Some hours before, she may refuse her usual food. She may assume a persistent and worried expression on her face, and if there is also a marked swelling of the vulva, accompanied by a clear mucous discharge, you can take it that proceedings are on the way.

Puppies are born one by one, each contained in its own membranous sac. The transparent-like material of this sac continues to cover the cord attached to the puppy's middle, through which it has been obtaining its nourishment from the mother, and at the end of this cord is attached the placenta or afterbirth, a dark liver-like substance. Puppy with cord and afterbirth are usually delivered together. With scissors snip the covering sac underneath the puppy's chin, and proceed to peel the sac or cawl from head downwards—it usually tends to shrivel up into the still adhering cord. Now with scissors cut the cord off at about three quarters of an inch from the puppy's navel. Give puppy to mother and promptly put afterbirth etc. in slop pail. Should afterbirth happen to remain behind, do not worry unduly at this stage, as it is likely to come away with the next puppy delivered. It is best to avoid the mother eating the afterbirth—if she doesn't see it she will not want it.

Sometimes it happens that a puppy in its little membranous sac appears emerging from the vulva as a dark bladder-like object through the transparent covering, half stuck and unable to get further. Take the soft Turkish towelling you have ready for the purpose, and with a firm hold of as much of the puppy in sac as you can get, pull steadily but firmly downward towards ground level, which is the natural direction of all animal parturition. In this way the cord is less likely to snap, and the whole stands a

Ch. Nova Horace, bred and owned by Mrs. U. Porritt.

better chance of coming away intact, i.e. puppy still in sac with cord and afterbirth attached.

After the mother has settled down comfortably with her litter, and one can feel assured there are no more to come, she should be left to rest with them. Quiet tidying up can start. The afterbirths are counted, to make sure they correspond in number with the puppies delivered.

About two hours later a coat can be put on the bitch, and she can be taken outdoors to relieve herself. She should be accompanied by someone she knows, as she may still be subject to some nervous reaction. In the meantime the puppies can be handed back into their own warm box. Do not have them handled by any other than the person who has handled them and attended to the bitch during her whelping.

While the bitch is still out, the whelping box can be quickly cleared out of soiled bedding, and changed for fresh, dry bedding, and the whelps replaced in time for the bitch's return. When settled with them again she should be given a good drink of the warm milk food she is having. For the first twenty-four hours at least after whelping, she should be fed on warm liquids every two to three hours. After this she can start some solid food again. Rabbit, fowl or fish at first, with stale brown bread soaked in warm gravy or meat stock. At the third day she can return to her usual meals and meat diet, but meat and milk should be of generous proportions to help her nourish her litter as well as herself.

"Carnivora," a colored 1880 print by Henry J. Johnson. From the Flamholtz collection.

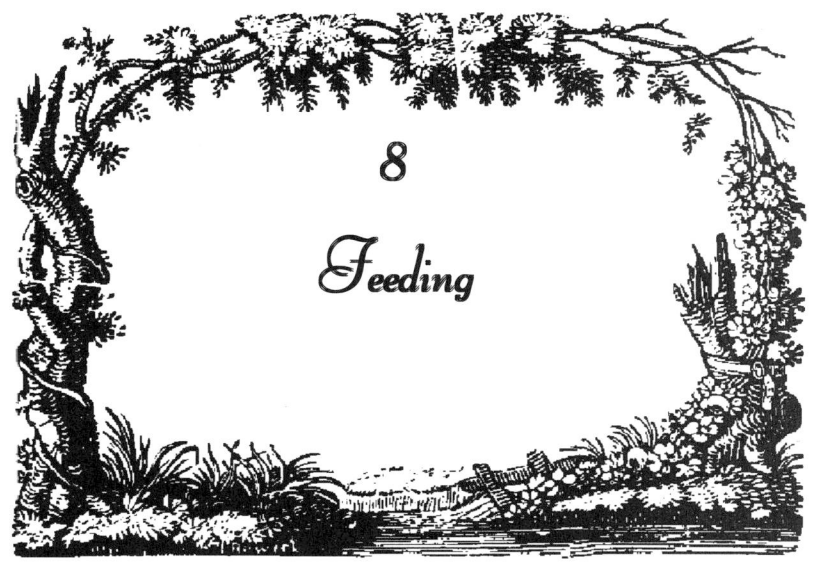

8
Feeding

(EDITOR'S NOTE: Some of the material contained in this chapter may be outdated. It is advisable to consult your veterinarian for appropriate information.)

S a general rule it has been found best for Pugs to start weaning at three weeks old. But it must be done gradually and systematically. The idea being more to *teach them how* to eat other food, than to make them actually eat and imbibe this alien food, as it will seem to them at first. Quite often the mother may be a valuable show bitch, and in any case it is a pity to allow her to be pulled out unduly by her bunch of lusty puppies if it is not really necessary for them, and undesirable for her. A bitch need not be balked of benefiting from all her maternal functions, and if she is properly done by, she should recover and indeed return to the show ring with her charms enhanced. A bitch who is left to be submerged by what Dickens has called 'These melancholy domestic circumstances', until even Nature finally dries her up in wrath, will soon look anything but like the show bitch she was, and more like Mrs. Micawber, 'A thin and faded lady, not at all young . . . with

a baby at her breast . . . one of twins . . . I hardly ever saw both the twins detached from Mrs. Micawber at the same time. One of them was always taking refreshment.'

As long as the puppies are sucking, the lacteal supply may continue to flow, but it will gradually decrease in quality and quantity. At the same time the growing puppies' demands become ever more insistent, with consequent strain on the poor bitch. All this can be avoided by properly weaning from three weeks old, as follows: on the first day, while the mother is outdoors, or in another room, try each puppy in turn with some warm milk, or the milk food they will be having. Place the saucer on the floor. They may waddle up to play and investigate. Let each one be shown the milk, and have his little head bobbed into the saucer. Some may dip a tongue in, others may actually take a lap, and there may be one who flatly refuses to be cajoled at all. On no account force them, whatever happens. So long as each puppy has had a lesson, and an equal amount of attention, the first weaning lesson has been accomplished for the day.

Next day the same programme, but this time there are two weaning lessons, at a mealtime interval. On the third day three similar weaning lessons. Scraped raw meat can be intro-

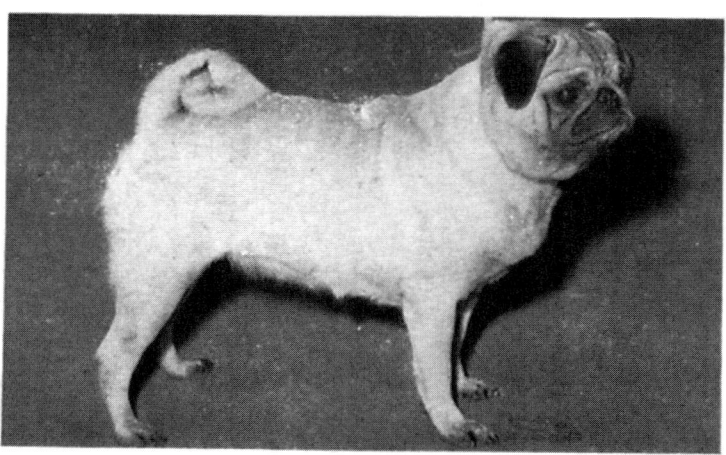

Miss M. Varley's Ch. St. Olam Shindy, bred by Mr. W. D. Joslin.

duced for the middle lesson on the fourth day. The other two lessons as before with the milk food only. The puppies must not be forced to eat. After a lesson or two on these lines, they will soon show they like the smell of meat, like all dogs.

If you work on this system, keeping to regular balanced rule, rather showing them *how* to eat, than making them eat, they will start eating and lapping quite naturally by themselves. Some may learn quicker than others, but they will soon all be toeing the line, and if they each systematically get the same attention, they will quite naturally by themselves begin to eat of the proffered food, all more or less at the same time, and so they go ahead.

Once they know how to eat, you can start introducing other foods, such as cereals in the first early breakfast feed, cod liver oil, stale brown breadcrumbs and meat stock with their meat. All this time the mother's milk should still be available, though, if the weaning process is going as it should, her milk will be gradually decreasing on its own.

By this method any normal healthy Pug litter can be said to be weaned at five weeks old, even though the mother may still be sleeping with her puppies at night. When she feels her milk decreasing, and she *knows* the puppies are feeding well on ordinary food, she may show, sometimes in no uncertain manner, that she considers she has fulfilled her mission this time, and start to absent herself from the family more frequently, particularly at night time, when she may crave to return to the peaceful sleeping quarters of her maiden days. The bitch's reactions should be studied and respected. Never force her. It would be as wrong to shut her off from the puppies against her will, as it would be to shut her in with them if she wants to get away from a litter of five weeks and over. When the puppies are three to four weeks old, she may be encouraged to leave them for a short time daily, for the relaxation of a little walk beyond the garden.

PUPPY FEEDING

At five weeks old if they have been weaned as described, they can be safely wormed. (EDITOR'S NOTE: Consult your veterinarian for his advice on an appropriate worming schedule.) Once they have got over that, they should go on very well with five little meals a day at this stage. Breakfast 8-8:30 a.m. Elevenses 11 a.m. Dinner 12:30 p.m. Tea 5 p.m. Supper 7:45-8 p.m.

As with human babies, apart from the mother's milk, there are many different milk foods to choose from. The difference between bitch's milk and that of goats and cows can be appreciated at a glance by the analyses in *The Complete Dog Breeders' Manual* by Clifford Hubbard (Sampson Low & Company). Here is the table:

ANALYSES OF MILK

Animal	Sugar	Casein, etc.	Fat	Salts	Water
Dog	3.1	8.0	12.0	1.2	75.5
Goat	4.75	4.0	6.25	1.0	84.0
Cat	5.2	7.9	3.65	0.9	82.35
Cow	4.85	3.75	3.7	0.6	87.1
Sheep	4.95	4.7	5.2	0.7	84.45

From this will readily be seen how dog's milk differs from that of other animals, particularly in fat. For instance, bitch's milk is very much richer in fat content than goat's milk, which is the second highest in fat content of those listed, cow's milk coming lowest of all in fat content. I have been surprised to learn there are breeders who still wean their puppies on diluted cow's milk. A glance at the above table should show the error of so doing. If cow's milk is used it should never be diluted, but rather strengthened by adding to it another good milk food in powder form. Cow's milk can be advantageously used to make milk puddings, semolina, ground rice etc., and for the puppies' custard puddings, which can be quite frequent. Some of the well-known milk foods especially manufactured for puppies have been proved to be most successful. Sherley's Lactol for instance has stood the test of time, and still retains its high reputation today, as the premier puppy milk food.

Pugs prefer their food and milk drinks fed just warm. With puppies being weaned off, this is even more important, as their food and drink should never be chill. While they are

Ch. Markendon Bengy, bred and owned by Mrs. M. B. Kendrick.

still learning about raw meat, they will actually swallow very little, but once they get a real appetite for it, it is time to mix it well with stale brown breadcrumbs or rusked brown bread soaked in meat stock. Place rusk or rusks in pie dish, cover with meat stock, put in oven for about half-an-hour, until the rusk has swelled and absorbed the stock juice, when ready mix the scraped raw meat (or mince or fish or whatever else they are having) with the hot rusk in a pie dish, divide into portions for each puppy's little plate, and feed to them while warm.

There are many puppy biscuit meals on the market. I have found, however, that nothing is so consistently good and reliable to mix with their meat etc. than whole-meal brown bread, crumbled up, on the stale side. Later the same, well rusked in the oven and soaked as advised for the smaller puppies, and later in the form of crumbs, which are made by putting the baked rusks through the largest knife in the mincing machine. This latter form is ideal for the adults too, as their staple cereal food to mix with their meat.

Most of the well-known cereal breakfast foods—Cornflakes, Puffed Wheat, Rice Crispies—are most useful for the puppies' breakfast. Oatmeal has been found altogether too overheating for Pugs. As for the many forms of biscuit meal, I have found nothing which so ideally suits the Pug as the brown bread, and rusks from this, as regular ballast with their daily meat meal. If one of the biscuit makes is used, it is best to have one not containing more than two ingredients, i.e. biscuit and dried meat, and more wholesome too than a biscuit meal consisting of several different ingredients. I have seen meal with as many as five ingredients, counting the biscuit meal. Why, for instance, so much dried meat, egg substance, charcoal etc. when fresh meat and eggs are available?

Sometimes when the puppies are eight weeks old, a good puppy meal, small grade, dried meat and biscuit only, can be usefully fed for supper and extra fresh meat added if desirable. Boiling meat stock is poured over the meal and when the liquid is absorbed, mix in the fresh meat and dole out warm into each little plate. The same meal, but without the added meat, can also be fed for a supper to adults who have already had their meat allowance during the day.

Everyone has their own opinion, and I hope I may not be considered too much of a killjoy, when I say I prefer to have my Pugs used to exercising their teeth regularly on hard dry biscuits than on bones, at any rate after early puppyhood, when they join the adults. Unless each dog can be separated, bones are certain to become 'a bone of contention', and fighting and injury may result. Bones do not suit all dogs, and given in between meals they are apt to spoil the appetite for the next meal. Pugs need some hard tackle, like all dogs, for the good of their teeth. Hard, dry dog biscuits can be given nightly after their suppers, or for their suppers. The habit should be formed early. The pups should be started at eight weeks old, with pieces of plain sweet biscuit as supplied for humans.

The author's Ch. Silvio of Swainston.

Miss E. H. McNair's homebred Ch. Geranium of Aynsley and Mrs. W. Clough's Ch. It's It of Cedarwood.

Soon they can go onto Spratt's Ovals fed in split halves, until they have learned to scrunch, and can safely take the biscuit whole. Adult Pugs can have six to eight Spratt's Ovals nightly. It is best to feed the biscuits by hand, and in turn, as Pugs enjoy this kind of community feeding, and it is good training in manners towards each other.

ADULT FEEDING

Most root vegetables, except potatoes, are good for Pugs. If cooked they should be well mashed. Scraped raw carrot, finely chopped well cleaned lettuce leaves, and parsley are all good—the latter, chopped finely, can be fed with their fish. Some Pugs find raw greens (spinach, cabbage, sprouts, etc.) either too strong or hard to digest. Cook these first, with little water, and chop finely.

Many Pugs show a marked fondness for fruit of all kinds. There is no reason why they shouldn't have fruit as a change from vegetables occasionally. Orange juice can be given with advantage, also tomato juice. This fondness for fruit is known in other breeds of dog of Oriental origin, which suggests some distant hereditary factor. In lands where meat and other food for dogs was not easily obtainable, but climatic conditions produced an abundance of fruit, the ancestors of the Oriental breeds probably became habituated to this diet and may well have passed on the predilection to their descendants.

I have seen a Pug enjoy a Cox's orange pippin as much as any small boy. When this particular dog gets an apple, he will carry it in his mouth until he finds someone willing to peel it for him, when he will lay it down before them until the job is done. There are some disadvantages, though, in this love of fruit. Should you happen to have a few fruit trees in your garden, your Pugs will busily collect the windfalls and proceed to devour them. Apples are not so bad. The trouble is the stone fruit, plums, damsons and cherries, which some Pugs swallow 'ad lib', stones and all! Too much fruit upsets their tummies, and the stones can be seriously upsetting to the digestive organs, and even dangerous. Some extra diligence in the garden regarding picking of fruit and collecting of windfalls may be indicated, but where dogs are not allowed free access to the gardens or orchards, and are penned in kennel runs, the trouble need not arise.

With the exception of puppies, pregnant or nursing bitches or Pugs on diet for specific purposes, it has been found that they neither care for nor require breakfast. Their first meal of the day should be their principal one containing their daily meat allowance. I give mine about 12:30 p.m. Raw meat is very good, and when freshly available should be mixed with cooked meat, which I have found the most successful with Pugs, because strange as it may seem, some Pugs are not so keen on raw meat as one would expect; but it usually gets gobbled up with the rest if mixed with cooked meat. At 5 p.m., each Pug gets some rather stale sponge cake, or better still home made rice cake, in pieces in his plate, fed dry, followed by a good drink of warm milk.

Supper at about 7:45 p.m. Hard biscuits for all—Spratt's Ovals, fed by hand, about eight each. Before biscuits, puppies over six and under twelve months, and others who are requiring feeding up, may have a small supper of dog biscuit meal, or one of the breakfast cereals with meat stock, and fed warm.

9
Management

ITH the Pug, wise and kindly rearing including a reasonable amount of regular discipline certainly pays good dividends, particularly if he is intended to do his bit in the world as show dog and breeder. Even as a pet his owner will get more satisfaction from him if he is a credit to his upbringing. Those who can afford to have proper kennels and runs constructed will likewise have extra help. Such kennels should be constructed with good means for heating in the winter. For bedding I find there is nothing more hygienic, comfortable and practical than the wood-wool sold in compressed hundredweight bales or half-bales. I always use this, though my Pugs are house dogs.

As for the smaller kennel which keeps no more than six dogs, sometimes less, I would recommend keeping Pugs as disciplined house dogs for best results: always assuming they are intended for show and breeding, as well as pets. Keeping them organized as house dogs, I believe to be the happiest compromise between spoiling them as pets and relegating them to live away from the house in kennels, be those kennels ever so grand and modern. But if the house Pugs are to be used for breeding and exhibiting, they should have their own room, one devoted to them only. If people can indulge in a music room or a studio, why not a dog room?

The floor of the dog room should be covered with a good, strong linoleum, not the shiny, slippery kind. A good cork lino is the best, one which will stand frequent scrubbing. In this room there can be cupboards for medicines, grooming implements etc. A small chest-of-drawers is useful too for coats, collars, leads, toys and show-pen curtains. A permanent bench can be erected in the dog-room for grooming. They can have their day boxes or baskets in here. It should be a fair sized room so that part of it can be partitioned off for small puppies, by wire and wood made panels, which can be removed, and hung up on hooks, when not in use.

Only too often, partly because the kitchen may be considered the warmest room in the house, one is tempted to keep the Pugs in it, which is far from the best thing for show dogs. Accidents are more prone to happen in kitchens, besides the proximity of food, which creates the ever ready temptation to give them tid-bits, a handicap to discipline from the start.

KENNELLING

Where a house dog sleeps at night has a greater bearing on that dog's character and temperament, not to mention the nervous system, than is generally realized.

Each Pug should have his own shut-in kennel to sleep in at night. There are many advantages making this worthwhile. For instance, a dog who is used to a shut-in kennel at night will not object to being in his pen at a show. He will also similarly not object to being put in a closed travelling box or hamper when journeys have to be undertaken. I have found it best to have the kennels in another part of the house, and not in the dog room where they spend the day. This not only gives more space in the dog room, but makes a change for them and the dog room can get a good airing during the night. Dogs trained to sleep in their house

HOUSE KENNEL

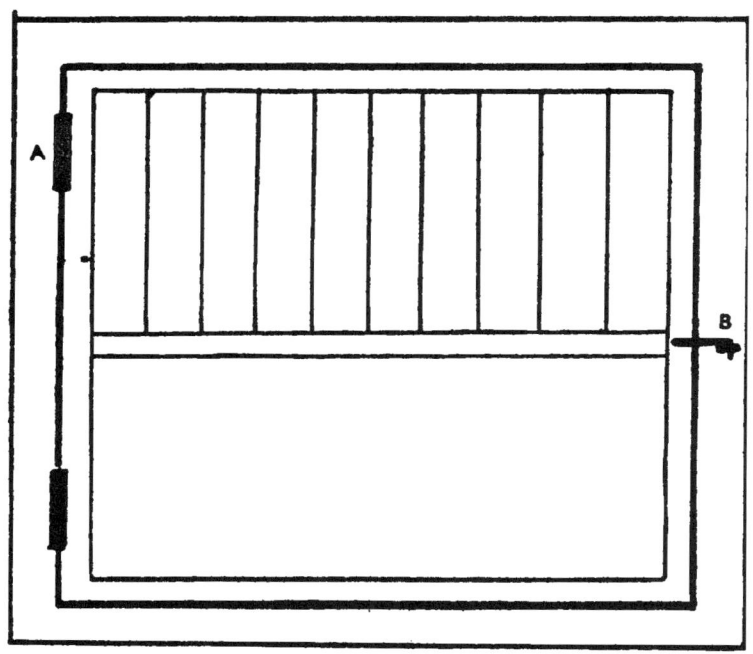

BATTEN

A. Door hinges.   B. Iron hook and eye for door.

$\frac{3}{16}"$ thick iron bars for window. Iron handles nailed on each side of kennel, for lifting (optional). Top and Bottom $21\frac{3}{4}" \times 22"$. Sides $22" \times 22"$. Back and Front $21\frac{3}{4}" \times 22"$. Two battens at bottom to raise kennel $3"$ off ground. $\frac{1}{2}"$ thick wood, except bottom (floor) which should be $\frac{3}{4}"$, as also for door.

kennels are perfectly warm and cosy throughout the night, requiring no artificial heating, even during the coldest winter months. The argument, how is a dog to be a guard if he is shut in a kennel can be discarded, at least so far as Pugs are concerned. It has been proved that a fastened-in dog at night can make as much noise at the onset of unusual sounds as one who is allowed to run loose. In any case, it is presumed that the Pug or Pugs are not being primarily kept as watch dogs, and if the ultimate aim is for show and breeding, it stands to reason that their general health must be the first consideration. Without health there can be no real beauty. Healthy, undisturbed sleep at night is a most important part of good conditioning.

Mrs. I. Walker's homebred Ch. Tynestad Singaria.

The house kennel should not be used during day time so that the dog will associate it with night time only. A thick layer of folded newspaper should be placed in the bottom of the kennel, and then a good supply of wood-wool bedding. This can be teazed up daily, when the Pugs are let outdoors (which should not be later than 7 a.m.) after which they return to the general dog-room. The bedding should be changed and the kennels given a good airing at least once every three weeks.

EXERCISE

Like all dogs Pugs profit from and enjoy a daily walk, part of which should be taken on the lead, and on hard roads, which should help to minimise the rather disagreeable recurrence of claw-cutting, to which many Pugs show such an aversion. They should also be taken somewhere grassy in parks or fields where they can safely be let off the lead for part of the time.

But as a breed they do not require an inordinate amount of exercise. An hour's daily walk is sufficient, and even this can be curtailed or cancelled altogether during hot summer weather with advantage, particularly if they have a good sized, safely enclosed garden to play and roam about in. The system of running them as house dogs, though keeping them to their own quarters, makes it easy to organize set times to let them out in the garden. This together with regular feeding times, conduces towards health creating habits of bodily digestion and elimination. Last thing at night, first thing in the morning, after each meal, etc. and, of course, in good weather they can be outdoors for longer periods at a time. If they are run this way they should be used to going out in any weather, at their regular times, if only to relieve themselves always providing they are thoroughly well dried with a good, rough towel before being allowed to settle down indoors again. Naturally when bitches come in season, they must be kept apart from the dogs, in another room in the house during the day time, and their night kennels must not be in the same room in which the dogs are sleeping.

HOUSE TRAINING

Pugs run on the house dog system described will almost automatically become house trained. The best principle in house training is to allow every opportunity from the earliest days to be clean, and avoid starting off with dirty habits, which so often have to be painfully un-learnt later. For the first few weeks of their life a good mother Pug will make it her business to keep her 'babies' spotlessly clean. At about three weeks when they start coming out of the whelping box and indulging in some venturesome waddling about, training in house manners can begin.

I have found the sawdust tray not only to be the most successful method for all concerned, but also the most pleasant.

The tray should be made of some galvanized metal measuring 5'-7 1/2" long, 2'-8" wide and 2" deep. The size, which may seem large, will be found more useful at this stage than a smaller one. Clean sawdust (pine for preference) is not hard to obtain. Sometimes a kind butcher will supply it. A small rake and shovel should be kept handy, to rake over wet patches, and shovel up stools from the sawdust. The whole tray should be changed for a fresh supply of sawdust once a week. As soon as the puppies come out of the whelping box, they should be encouraged to go in the tray, and praised when they use it. It is not too early to teach them that the tray, and *not* their nursery floor is the proper place, by pointing out a lapse to the offender, giving him a small tap, and a good growl, and holding him for half-a-minute in the tray. It is surprising how quickly they learn. Warm water and disinfectant and a wrung-out cloth should ever be ready to wipe up any puddles on the floor, with a supply of newspaper always available.

With a regular scrub out of the puppy-room once a week, and plenty of fresh air, there should never even be a whiff of a smell. Once the puppies have got the hang of the sawdust tray,

Mrs. M. Cumming's Ch. Hazelbridge.

providing it is made easily accessible to them from their whelping box and day box or basket, they will soon cease wetting and fouling their bedding, and acquire the tray habit instead. When they are allowed out-of-doors on grass in the garden, or in pens, they will soon find there are only two places where they are permitted to relieve themselves, i.e. out-of-doors, or in sawdust tray.

Later if a puppy or puppies are to be kept, and the time comes to promote them to join the older Pugs in the general dog-room, it may be best at first to have a smaller sawdust tray in a corner of the dog-room in case of emergencies, but now the puppy must learn to go out with the older dogs. The time to remove the temporary tray for good must be left to the owner's discretion, but when it does happen the puppy should be well prepared to cope with the new idea that now there is only one way left to relieve himself, which is out-of-doors like the big dogs. Even older puppies may have to be let outdoors more frequently than the older dogs at first. Always remember the golden rule in house training, that 'Prevention is better than Cure'.

GROOMING AND BATHING

The necessity of regular grooming, not only for the show dog but also for the house pet, cannot be over emphasized. A well groomed dog is every bit as pleasing an individual to live with as a well groomed human being. However, grooming the Pug need not be the daily chore which is practically a necessity for longer-coated dogs. Indeed it has been found that daily brushing and combing after a time in some cases is inclined to over-stimulate the Pug's skin, and actually do more harm than good. Some Puggists have made this an excuse to neglect the grooming of their Pugs, and almost to pride themselves on the breed requiring little or no grooming at all. This is a great pity, and such Pugs are always at a disadvantage when coming up against others who are regularly groomed.

A thorough, regular grooming once a week should never be omitted, when eyes and ears are attended to, claws examined, etc. By such overall attention regularly once a week, one stands a better chance of spotting any incipient trouble of the skin or otherwise in good time to check it. Pugs should be placed on a bench or table to be groomed. This teaches them early to get used to being handled on a table, which is often required nowadays by some show judges.

The late Mrs. C. M. Crawford's Ch. Fordcraw Beauty.

In the ordinary event, particularly if they are house dogs, and their living quarters are kept up to the standard of human cleanliness and they are regularly groomed once a week, Pugs do not require a lot of baths. A good bath between the end of Spring and the start of Summer, and another at the end of September before the Winter months set in is all that is usually required, except, of course, before a show, when a good bath is a most important item of a Pug's pre-show programme.

If an early morning start is to be made for the show, a fawn Pug should have been bathed and groomed for show the day before. The black Pug should be bathed four days before the show, to allow for return after the bath of the natural lustre to the coat, but he should receive his last show grooming at home, as near as possible to his start for the show. I have found Wright's Coal Tar soap to be the very best both for skin and effect.

Pugs as a rule enjoy having a bath. The fact is they much enjoy being the centre of human attention, and there is no reason why the bathing procedure should be fraught with unpleasantness for them. They should always, whatever the time of the year, be bathed indoors, and they must never be let outdoors until at least an hour after they have been proved to be bone dry. They should be vigorously dried with good, clean rough towels, in a warm room with some extra heating whilst drying off. Do not be in a hurry to turn him outdoors after he has had a bath. It is a wise precaution to wait until after he has had one of his regular meals before letting him outdoors, as he is less likely to catch cold after recently being fed.

AILMENTS

A few words on the most common that beset the Pug may not be inopportune here, but for a really good study of dog ailments I would refer you to *The Book of the Dog* (Nicholson & Watson, Ltd.), wherein the 'Accident and Disease Nursing Treatment' section is well written by a veterinary surgeon of wide repute. (EDITOR'S NOTE: Be sure to consult your veterinarian for up-to-date medical advice.)

Eyes.

As with other small dogs of Oriental origin such as the Pekingese and the Japanese Spaniels, who all possess the large, round, somewhat protruding eyes, this orb, so beautiful and characteristic, can also be a source of anxiety. The very nature of its protrusion or 'popping out' effect causes it to be more vulnerable to injury.

One chief trouble is the corneal ulcer. These ulcers can happen through injury, by accident, or even through some infection, or catching cold. It is good to note however that many Pugs go right through life with eyes unscathed.

These ulcers often leave scars on the cornea behind them. They are more prevalent in early puppyhood, particularly those due to external injuries. Should there remain a scar on the cornea, in most cases one can count on this showing less as the Pug gets older because the head and eyes increase in size, but the scar, of course, remains the same. The original size of the scar depends on the extent of the ulcer, and on its subsequent treatment. Nowadays, particularly since the last war, the veterinary profession has become increasingly skilful in canine ophthalmics. If your Pug gets a bad eye it is safest to call in your vet and treat according to his directions. In the meantime, however, should you notice a puppy's eyes watering unduly, and appearing half-closed, or the puppy rubbing it, you could proceed to bathe both eyes with warmed Optrex eye lotion, using cotton wool, after which squeeze a drop of warmed Argyrol 5% solution into the bad eye, from a small piece of cotton wool soaked in the solution. Afterwards dry the outer eyes and face well with dry cotton wool. If taken in time this simple treatment has often warded off the incidence of an ulcer altogether. (EDITOR'S NOTE: Consult your veterinarian to learn about current veterinary practices.)

Considering this tendency towards delicacy of Pugs' eyes, it is well worth while taking the precaution of keeping them clean and healthy from earliest puppyhood. From six weeks old puppies' eyes should be bathed regularly every morning with warmed Optrex, or any other reliable eye lotion, and dried afterwards with cotton wool. As puppies grow older, join the adults and get the weekly grooming in their turn, they will only require eye washing once a week. If a Pug's eyes are all right, they should only require a once-aweek eye wash with warm water. Always dry the outer eyes well afterwards. Anything chill should never come in contact with the eyes.

Ears.

Pugs are no more subject to ear canker or aural troubles than other dogs. If the simple precaution is taken regularly once a week of putting a pinch of boracic powder inside each ear, and working it firmly and gently, with a finger into the inner crevices of the ear, the incidence of canker can be avoided, and your Pug's ears will always be as fresh as little roses. At bathing times care should be taken to avoid any water entering the ears. It is the astringent action of the boracic powder, as well as its cleansing and soothing properties, that make it so valuable an aid in the care of the inner ears.

Cysts.

Interdigital cysts (swelling in between the toes) are not uncommon in Pugs. Dogs who are afflicted with them often have a recurrence which, together with the theory that these cysts may be of eczematic origin, has contributed towards the opinion that there is some hereditary tendency in certain individuals. It may be found that such dogs are having too rich a diet: too much fat meat and an insufficiency of green vegetables. Plenty of exercise and fresh air in between the incidence of a cyst is indicated. Nothing is more annoying than for a Pug to spring one of these cysts before a show. He is only too likely to be lame for the time being, which is such a severe handicap in the ring that he is better left at home.

Lancing of these cysts by veterinary surgeons was given up years ago as being useless. The swellings are hard and there is no core. The best treatment is hot fomentation, after which, when the paw is thoroughly dry, apply a generous application of Iodex ointment all over the swelling, and also in between the other toes. Place the dog on a bench or table, make him stand the bad paw in a basin containing as hot water as he can bear with a drop of Dettol in it; lift the paw out nf water and squirt a steady jet of water against the cyst. Do this several times. Use a small self-filling bulbous rubber plunger for the purpose. This has a most beneficial effect. Each time the plunger is refilling, let the dog stand the paw again in the basin. Dry the paw by holding it wrapped in a warm Turkish towel. When dry apply the Iodex. At night, after he has had his last outing, is the best time to do the treatment, so that he gets to bed and rests in his kennel immediately afterwards.

I have found this treatment sometimes disperses a threatening cyst altogether. It will help to clear it away sooner, and it can always be relied upon to relieve the pain of the swelling.

Wrinkle Rash

This is more a condition that need not arise than a disease, though it can become quite a worry. Its proper name is erythema, and it is a red inflamed condition of the skin usually unaccompanied by spots or pimples, which sets up in the deep wrinkles on Pugs' faces. The trouble can be prevented by taking regular precautions once a week at grooming time. This skin between the wrinkles is tender, due to a combination of moisture and the lack of direct contact with fresh air. At grooming time after doing the eyes, open out the wrinkles on the face and above the nose, and dry thoroughly in between them with dry cotton wool. Dry by padding and pressing, never rub, as the skin is so tender it can easily be further irritated. Now leave it while you groom the dog. Last thing, take a pinch of boracic powder and spread and press it in well all along and inside the wrinkles. Only if the rash should already be present, it is best before starting with the boracic powder to thoroughly clean the sore parts by swabbing them with cotton wool dipped in warm water containing a drop of Dettol, and then thoroughly dry inside the wrinkles with dry cotton wool.

Mange.

There are two kinds, both due to a parasite—the common or sarcoptic mange, and follicular mange. Of the two, the common should be curable within three weeks, though it takes some time for the hair to grow again, providing the kennel hand is prepared to work hard and consistently: the cure lies in the destruction of the parasite (which, when seen through the microscope is a bug-shaped creature) which fastens itself fairly near the surface of the skin and fixes its eggs to the hairs on the dog's body. Common mange is highly contagious by reason of its being near the surface, and it is quite active and will move from one dog to another. Warmth inclines the mites to move, as when an infested dog lies curled up and close to others. The fact of common mange being so easily contagious also makes it easier to cure. The parasite, being nearer the surface, is more readily accessible to destructive agents in the form of medicated baths and dressings.

Follicular mange is a more serious type altogether. Fortunately it is neither so common as the other type nor so contagious to other dogs. The parasite responsible (which is rather smaller and of a fishlike shape when seen through the microscope) burrows deeply beneath the skin surface, which at the same time unfortunately causes the greatest difficulty in getting at it with destructive agents.

There are so many varied forms of treatment and dressings that it is best to follow the instructions of your veterinary surgeon. As already stated, in both forms of mange the cure lies in a campaign of unremitting battle, giving the parasite no peace until it is thoroughly routed. Have your vet take a scraping from the skin for examination under the microscope, which should reveal the parasite, if present, and whether it is the *Sarcoptes Scabiei Canis* (common mange parasite) or the *Demodex Folliculorum* (follicular mange parasite). This is the speediest and most conclusive method of diagnosis, because if the trouble is caused by a parasite it should be visible in the scraping under the microscope.

Needless to say, the safest precaution against any infestation of parasites is strict attention to cleanliness and hygiene of dogs and surroundings.

Worms.

The two most common are the round worm and the tape worm, the former showing rather an attachment for the Pug, though I believe that many adult Pugs who have round worms are often dogs who have never been properly cleared of this pest in early puppyhood.

Without a careful study of the life cycle of the round worm, it is impossible to explain why it is that round worms are present in nearly all puppies. Because of this it is advisable to worm all healthy puppies. (EDITOR'S NOTE: We now know that round worms may be passed in utero.

Many veterinarians recommend that only puppies with worms actually be wormed. Consult your veterinarian for advice.) Puppies who have started weaning as previously described can safely be wormed at five weeks old. There are many different worm medicines to choose from. Some of the latest and best are only obtainable through a veterinary surgeon, so it is a good plan when the time comes to ask your vet to prescribe. The same applies to the tape worm, which is likelier to favour adult dogs as hosts. Country dogs are generally more subject to tape worm than those who live in towns. Rabbit infested land is often a source of contraction. Worms are hostile to health and well being. If Pugs are properly wormed, there is no real reason why they should have a recurrence of the pest, and the practice of regular worming two or three times a year 'just in case the dog may have them' is not advocated for the Pug.

It may not be generally known that one can, if one wishes, send away a specimen of a dog's feces for an examination by a parasitologist. This can be done through your veterinary surgeon. The test reveals whether worm eggs are present or not, and may save all the worry to yourself, and stress to the dog, of unnecessary worming. (EDITOR'S NOTE: This is now a routine practice, performed in every veterinary office.)

Inoculation

Inoculation as a preventive against distemper, and hard pad, and other virus diseases, has become ever more universal since the last war, but it is still a burning subject of controversy with some whether to inoculate or not. (EDITOR'S NOTE: There is no longer any controversy about modern inoculations. They are routinely given to all dogs.) Usually members of the veterinary profession have no hesitation in answering in the affirmative. However much one may deplore the principle of using evil to cast out evil, yet if this provides the only reasonable chance of preventing great suffering and probable death, one may find it hard to reconcile one's conscience in denying this chance to the dog. British dogs are still the most prized in the world, and British people the greatest dog lovers. Our veterinary force and research workers are untiring in their efforts and never ceasing study to discover antidotes and improvements for fighting these cruel and killing scourges. Puppies can be inoculated now between three and four months or even younger, with one injection to last for life, and since this latest form has been in general use it must be admitted that within the last few years we hear and read less about epidemics of distemper and hard pad ravaging different parts of the country (and sometimes whole kennels getting wiped out) which was only too common a tragedy before.

10
Exhibiting

HOWING if taken seriously is more than a pastime, it is the way to become cultured in your breed. If not taken seriously, it is simply not worth the effort in expense and time involved, particularly nowadays. But even for those who can afford to pay for loss as well as gain, it is worth while carefully considering whether you are made of the right stuff to stand rebuffs and disappointments on the way.

If you are the right sort, all is worth it for the sake of your breed and your dogs. The joy of a first well merited success helps to spur one on to further efforts, and one soon discovers what an absorbingly interesting occupation it is. Apart from the dog cult, the amount to be learnt about human nature in all its vagaries at dog shows, has to be experienced to be believed. In the chapter on breeding it was said that the nonexhibitor pet Pug owner's destiny might be an easier one, and no one can gainsay that it may not be a very happy one, but it will lack the interest and competition of the show world.

The aim of showing is primarily to improve your breed by obtaining the opinion of experts on your exhibits, seeing other people's dogs, noting the winners and, above all, trying to assess

Mrs. D. Bunn's Ch. Philip of Modelhouse.

the judge's point of view, even if you fail to reconcile it with your own. Remember, especially if your show days are fairly early, it is possible the judge may know best after all.

A word may be said here on an aspect which is sometimes puzzling to the beginner at shows, and that is the differing opinions of the different judges. First because it is as well to be prepared for what sometimes comes as an anti-climax, after perhaps an unexpected first success, to find your Pug placed top of his class, and at the very next show under another judge, lo and behold, the same dog is left out altogether! Only a little calm reflection will show that if judges were all of the same opinion, dog showing would soon come to a full stop altogether, and it is the general consensus of opinion over a period of time that eventually proves the merit of any dog in the show ring. It is something indeed even if Miss A., the judge this time, did not care for your dog, that Mr. B., on the contrary, at the last show liked him so much as to put him top of his class. So keep on trying. There never was a truer adage than: 'You can't keep a good dog down'. Granting the fact that different judges are of different persuasions, in the long run if your dog is a good one, and you keep on trying, he will get his just due. His merits will become known—his 'ups' will be more frequent than his 'downs'.

And as time goes on you yourself will grow to know more about the judges, who are only human after all. For instance, through your own observation, you will become aware by one judge's placings that he usually puts up larger Pugs, or smaller Pugs, or prefers lighter-coloured fawns to the darker shade. On the other hand, another judge may show by his placing a preference for the correct dark coloured eye, or be extremely particular about a tight curled twist, etc. Remember, you may enter your exhibit at any show, under any judge, so you are free to choose one whom you think may like your Pug. Indeed, this is only part of your own job as an exhibitor, in the right way of running your dog's show career. You are his manager, and it behoves you to learn all you can, and keep your wits about you, just as the manager runs his film star in another kind of show world. Pugs as a rule make splendid little show dogs. They greatly appreciate all the admiration and praise they can get, and will usually make a very good show of themselves, if only they are shown how.

The right training of the show dog from the start is important. It should be as great a thrill to its owner to watch the evolution of a promising puppy into a good show dog as is experienced by any creative artist in the accomplishment of his aim. Fortunate is the owner who can start from earliest days. The tiniest puppy, even before he has learnt to wear a collar, can be encouraged to stand still, pose, and the little beggar will soon learn how to look his bewitching best in return for human approval, which he loves.

He should first be taught to wear a small, flat and never tight house collar during day time from eight weeks old. At twelve weeks he can start his 'school' in the 'infant' class by being given a few minutes' daily lessons in the garden on collar and lead. Never pull or drag a puppy by the lead. Let him get used to the lead attached to the collar until he gets to take it for granted that you are holding the other end, though it will be some time before he goes for regular walks on collar and lead with the older dogs. It is an excellent thing, besides forming the foundation of his show ring training, to give him the sense of discipline of knowing how to do 'collar and lead' from his earliest days.

Later, when the time comes for his first show, he can start being put through his paces for the show ring, and here let it be stated that every show dog, no matter how experienced, should have his daily practice at home, in an improvised show ring, for three weeks before his every show—just as no human actor could be expected to perform his role on the stage properly without regular rehearsals beforehand. Fortunately, however, the show dog's daily practice should not be prolonged beyond about five minutes daily. The aim is to induce him to enjoy the idea of showing, and never to weary him, which would only defeat the purpose by getting him fed up with the whole idea. A dog who has been properly trained and knows what is expected of him beforehand is far more likely to make a better impression in the show ring than one who through sheer bewilderment looks as if he doesn't even know how to go on the lead properly, let alone how to show himself off to best advantage.

Show practice beforehand is as necessary to the handler as his exhibit. The handler should make it his business to get acquainted with the principal moves required in the show ring, which are quite simple and straightforward. At first the judge usually stands in the middle watching exhibitors walking their dogs around the ring. The dogs always on the inside so that the judges can see them. The judge will have a ring steward with him to help him direct the exhibitors where to stand, and hand out the prize cards at the end of the class.

Having seen the dogs moving all together, the judge will pick out any exhibitor and direct him to walk his dog across the ring and back again. Unless he asks you to repeat this move, when you return to the judge you should be prepared to make your Pug stand still with his tail tightly curled, in short looking his absolute best for the judge's approval. Your dog must also be prepared to allow the judge to handle him about the body and head. Some judges ask you to lift the dog up in your arms, and others like to handle the exhibits on a bench or table in the ring. All of which you and your Pug should be prepared for. When the judge has finished with you, you will be directed to a spot in the ring where you will be expected to stay, and make way for the next exhibit to be put through his paces as was yours. Sometimes the judge will call you back, if he wants to see your Pug again to compare him with one of the others. He may ask you and the other exhibitor to run your Pugs side by side across the ring and back again, in which case the dogs should be run together side by side, and their handlers on the outside.

Mrs. W. Stanley Young's Ch. Archibald of Rydens, with two of his friends, all home bred and under one year old.

Always cultivate a pleasant manner in the ring, keeping your own and your dog's deportment in mind. Remember, as well as the judge and your competitors, you are always in the presence of your public, like any other performer. When the judge is examining other exhibits, you can let yourself and exhibit relax slightly, as long as you don't allow yourself to assume any vagueness of pose, so that you are promptly ready, should the judge turn around and cast an eye in your direction, when it might be to your greatest advantage if your dog happened to be clearly visible and standing nicely.

Training for an outdoor show can happily take place in the garden. As for props in the ring, i.e. tid-bits or toys, the former are to be preferred as being not only more reliable, but less ostentatious. Means should be available indoors to improvise a training ring in case of bad weather and for the shows under cover.

When training and showing wear a coat or garment with two pockets, each pocket containing a sufficient supply of meat or cooked liver cut up very small so that when required you can produce a tid-bit from either side, whichever the most convenient, as quickly and unobtrusively as possible.

Although a Pug can be trained and put through his paces on his own, it is a good plan to have others, particularly experienced show dogs handled by someone else, to practise with him. This, besides getting him used to other dogs in the ring, will be invaluable in giving him the right idea, especially about getting a tid-bit himself if he is a good dog!

CLASSES

In every schedule you will find a list of defined classes offered and these are taken from the official list prepared by the Kennel Club. The smaller the show the fewer classes will be offered, of course, while at the Championship and other Open shows the classes scheduled will run from Puppy to Open Dog and Open Bitch. In the list that follows here it is to be understood that the word 'dogs' applies to both sexes, and that the classes may be duplicated at any one show, one being for dogs and the other for bitches.

DEFINITIONS OF CLASSES
(Vide Kennel Club Regulations for Definitions of Classes)

(EDITOR'S NOTE: These regulations applied to British shows and may no longer be current.)

PUPPIES UNDER SIX CALENDAR MONTHS OF AGE ARE NOT ELIGIBLE FOR ENTRY

A dog is not eligible for entry in Variety classes unless entered in Breed classes, where such classes are provided for which it is eligible.

A dog shall not obtain a Challenge Certificate unless it has won a prize in a class confined to its recognized breed or variety in which full prize money is offered and open to all exhibitors at the show in question, and unless it is in the show at the time the award is made.

In the case of a dog owned in partnership, and entered in Members' classes or competing for Members' Specials, each member of such partnership must at the time of entry be a member of such Association, Club or Society.

In estimating number of prizes won, all wins previous to the midnight preceding the day specified in the schedule for closing entries shall be counted when entering for any class. Equal awards shall count as a win for each dog so placed.

Wins in Variety classes do not count for entry in Breed classes, and a win not dependent on judging by breed points does not count. A Variety class is one in which more than one breed or variety of a breed can compete. A first prize does not include a first prize in Club Stakes or Special prize of whatever value. With this proviso the following are the definitions of certain classes:

Special Puppy—For dogs and bitches of six and not exceeding *nine* calendar months of age on the day of the show.

Puppy—For dogs and bitches of six and not exceeding *twelve* calendar months of age on day of show.

Junior—For dogs and bitches of six and not exceeding *eighteen* calendar months of age on day of show.

Maiden—For dogs or bitches which have not won a *first* prize of the value of £1 or more.

Novice—For dogs and bitches which have not won more than *two* first prizes each of the value of £1 or more.

Debutant—For dogs and bitches which have not won a *first* prize of the value of £2 or more.

Undergraduate—For dogs and bitches which have not won more than *two* first prizes each of the value of £2 or more.

>Note—No dog is eligible for entry in Maiden, Novice, Debutant and Undergraduate classes, which has won a Challenge Certificate or has obtained any award that counts towards the title of Champion under the Rules of any Governing Body recognized by the Kennel Club.
>When entering for Graduate, Post Graduate, Minor Limit, Mid Limit or Limit classes, exhibitors must count all first prize wins of £2 or more in the classes listed in the definitions whether these classes are restricted or not.

Graduate—For dogs and bitches which have not won more than *three* first prizes, each of the value of £2 or more in Graduate, Post Graduate, Minor Limit, Mid Limit, Limit or Open classes.

Post Graduate—For dogs or bitches which have not won more than *four* first prizes, each of the value of £2 or more, in Post Graduate, Minor Limit, Mid Limit, Limit or Open classes.

Minor Limit—For dogs and bitches which have not won *two Challenge Certificates* or more than two first prizes in all, each of the value of £2 or more, in Minor Limit, Mid Limit, Limit or Open classes, confined to the breed, at shows where Challenge Certificates were offered for the breed.

Mid Limit—For dogs and bitches which have not won *three Challenge Certificates* or more than four first prizes in all, each of the value of £2 or more, in Mid Limit, Limit or Open classes, confined to the breed, at shows where Challenge Certificates were offered for the breed.

Limit—For dogs and bitches which have not won *three Challenge Certificates under three different judges* or more than six first prizes in all, each of the value of £2 or more, in Limit or Open classes, confined to the breed, at shows where Challenge Certificates were offered for the breed.

Restricted Limit—Similar to a Limit class, except it is restricted to weight, colour, height, etc.

Open—For all dogs and bitches. If confined to a breed or variety, for all dogs of that breed or variety.

Restricted Open—Similar to Open class except that it is restricted as to weight, colour, height, or to Members of an Association.

Brace—For two exhibits (either sex or mixed) of one breed or variety belonging to the same exhibitor, each exhibit having been entered in some class other than Brace.

Team—For three or more exhibits (either sex or mixed) of one breed or variety belonging to the same exhibitor, each exhibit having been entered in some class other than Brace or Team.

11
Footnotes

1. When these strange new breeds first came to England the resemblance to Pugs was so apparent that they were often misnamed 'Peking Pugs' or 'Japanese Pugs.'

2. The reason for the frequent appearance of the Pug in Meissen porcelain is a curious one. The Elector of Saxony, who was the most important patron of Meissen, was also Grand Master of the Freemasons, and when the Pope excommunicated the Masons in Germany in 1736, they continued to function in an underground way as 'Mopsorden' or 'The Order of Pugs.' The Pu was their secret symbol and, at about the same time, ladies were first admitted to the Order. Count Brühl, managing director of the Meissen factory at its best period, had numerous Pugs, and the exquisite figures by Kaendler are probably of his dogs.

3. I use the term 'normal' as does Dr. G. M. Vevers to distinguish the common type of canine skull from the achondroplasic or short-faced type found among the Oriental Toys (see Vesey-FitzGerald, *The Book of the Dog,* pp. 12-13).

4. The Hon. Mrs. Lytton in her *Toy Dogs and their Ancestors,* 1911, makes a strong case for the theory that the original Toy Spaniels came to Italy from China at some very early date. King Charles Spaniels may have been introduced to England by Queen Catherine of Braganza with specimens imported from Japan to Portugal. The Emperor of Japan sent presents direct to the King of England as early as 1613; these articles, we are told, always formed part of an Imperial Japanese present: rice, dried fish and dogs. The Spaniels shown in the Italian painting of 1575 have a very Oriental look.

5. For an excellent discussion of the history of the Mastiff, one of the most interesting and beautiful of all breeds, see James Watson's very fully illustrated chapter in *The Dog Book,* 1906.

6. Pugs were often loosely called 'Dutch Mastiffs' in England in the middle of the later eighteenth century.

7. *The Pekingese Handbook,* 1951.

8. *Peking and the Pekingese,* 1865.

9. Their grand-daughter "Cloudy" was born in 1872.

10. The overland caravan trade route from China to Europe became established during the Han Dynasty, some hundred years before the Christian era. The word 'seras,' here translated 'Chinese,' is translated 'Tartar' in Vesey-FitzGerald's *The Domestic Dog,* but Strabo (who lived at the same time as Grattius) defines the word as only applying to the people who live in China. *(EDITOR'S NOTE: Many authorities believe that 'seras' should be translated as 'Tibetans,' and that the quote referred to pertains to the Tibetan Mastiff.)*

11. The Emperor Ling-Ti (A.D. 168-190) presented to his favourite dog the official hat and belt of the Hsien grade, the highest literary honour of the times. The hat measured 8 3/4"

high in front, 3 3/4" high behind, and 10" broad. Dogs raised by the Emperor were given the rank of Kai-Fu (Viceroy) and bitches ranks equivalent to those of wives of high officials.

12. Dr. W. Lockhart, writing in 1867 of 'the two kinds of Pug in China,' refers to one type being long-legged, and the other short-legged. It appears that "Lamb" and "Moss" were of the short-legged type, and the blacks imported by Lady Brassey and Mrs. Guyer (all of which showed white markings) were of the long-legged type. Dr. Lockhart adds: 'Sometimes in these dogs the eyes are so prominent that I have known a dog have one of his eyes snapped off by another dog in play.'

13. See pp. 9-14 and Pl. i of *The Pekingese Handbook,* 1951.

14. Motley and others confuse this dog with the small Spaniel sculptured at the foot of the William's tomb at Delft. But the Delft dog is far from 'snub-nosed' and obviously a different breed.

15. Other writers contradict Mr. Mayhew's account and say the Willoughby strain commenced from a Pug obtained from Vienna which originally belonged to a Hungarian Countess.

16. 'Her Majesty's black Pug had four white feet, a white shirt front and white lips, a very prominent skull, square jaw, long face and huge globular eyes—and was hideously cropped.' (*L.K.J.,* 1896). These white marks, as already stated, are characteristic of Chinese blacks and were not found at that date on English Pugs, fawn or black.

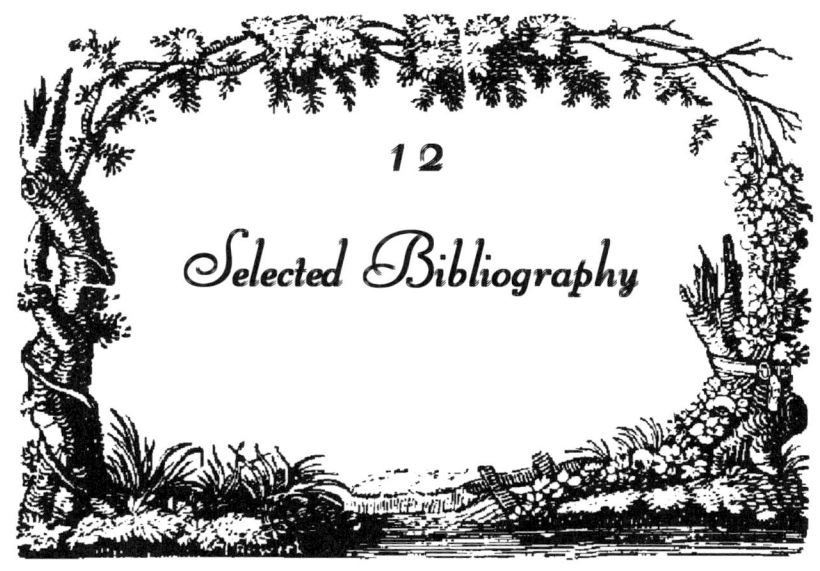

12
Selected Bibliography

It is hoped that this brief list will serve to recommend a selection of books in the English language which are particularly useful to students of this breed. Unless otherwise stated the dates given are those of first editions.

ALLEN, L. and ASTLEY, L. P. C.: *The Perfect Pekingese. A Monograph,* London, 1912.

ASH, E. C.: *Dogs: Their History and Development,* 2 volumes, London, 1927.
The Pekingese, London, 1936.

AYSCOUGH, F.: *The Autobiography of a Chinese Dog,* London, 1926.

BEILBY, W.: *The Dog in Australasia,* Melbourne, 1897. This scarce book is important in that it gives an illustrated chapter on the Pug in Australasia. Fawns were first imported into Tasmania in 1879 and Beilby tells in this book how they were distributed from the 'Apple Island' to the whole of the Australian continent.

BRASSEY, ANNIE, COUNTESS: *A Voyage in the Sunbeam,* London, 1878.

COLLIER, V. W. F.: *Dogs of China and Japan in Nature and Art,* London, 1921. This scarce book is invaluable to the serious student for its profound researches, scholarship and honest conclusions. Copiously illustrated (some plates are in colour) it is an essential work of reference in the study of eastern breeds.

CRYER, M. H.: *The Prize Pugs of America and England,* New York, 1891. This rare book gives valuable information about Pugs of the latter half of the nineteenth century in Britain and America, together with pedigrees.

DALZIEL, H.: *British Dogs: Their Varieties, History, Characteristics, Breeding, Management and Exhibition,* London, 1881. The second edition, 1888-97, is of three volumes. Dalziel's book shows the origins of the official Standard of the London Pug Club, which Standard was largely purloined, without acknowledgement, from the first edition of his book.

DE SALIS, H.: *Dogs: A Manual for Amateurs,* London, 1893.

DENLINGER, M. G.: *The Complete Pug,* Washington, 1947.

DIXEY, A. C.: *The Lion Dog of Peking,* London, 1931.

DUFF (see Gratius Faliscus).

EDWARDS, S. T.: *Cynographia Britannica,* London, 1800. One of the rarest of all dog books and the first to have hand coloured illustrations. The work was issued in parts and never completed.

GOLDSMITH, O.: *An History of the Earth and Animated Nature,* London, 1774.

GOODGER, W. S.: *The Pug: Its History and Origin,* Bradford, 1930.

GRATIUS FALISCUS: *Cynegeticon.* A Latin and English edition, entitled *Cynegeticon Gratti,* was edited by John W. and A. M. Duff, London, 1934.

GRESHAM (see Shaw, V. K.).

HACKENBROCH (see Untermeyer and Hackenbroch).

HONEY, W. B.: *Dresden China,* London, 1934. New edition, 1954.

HUBBARD, C. L. B.: *Dogs in Britain,* London, 1948.
An Introduction to the Literature of British Dogs, Ponterwyd, 1949.
The Pekingese Handbook, London, 1951.

HURRY, C.: *The Oracle Dog and the Sages,* London, 1954. A charming little book about "Sir Samuel Batholiver Stilton Pug"—just done for fun.

Hutchinson's Dog Encyclopedia, London, 1935. This three-volume work is interesting for its illustrations of early Pugs.

'IDSTONE' (see Pearce, T.).

KENDALL, H. R.: *International Dogs,* New York, no date.

LAUFER, B.: *Chinese Pottery of the Han Dynasty,* London, 1909. The section of this book by a great oriental scholar entitled 'Races of Dogs in Ancient China' (pp. 247-81) sheds new light not only on the origins of the Pug, Pekingese and Japanese Spaniel group, but also on those of the Mastiff and the Greyhound.

LE CLERK, G. L., COMTE DE BUFFON: *Histoire Naturelle,* Paris, 1749-1804.

LEE, R. B.: *A History and Description of the Modern Dogs of Great Britain and Ireland* (Non-Sporting Division), London, 1894.

LEIGHTON, R.: *The New Book of the Dog,* London, 1907 (also a deluxe edition of three volumes).
The Complete Book of the Dog, London, 1922.

LYTTON, Hon. Mrs. N.: *Toy Dogs and Their Ancestors,* London, 1911.

PEARCE, T. ('Idstone'): *The Dog,* London, 1872.

PIOZZI (see Thrale, H. L.).

PUGHE, L. J. E.: *Black Pugs: Hints on their Management,* Blackburn, 1905.

RAYMOND-MALLOCK, L. C.: *Toy Dogs,* Kenilworth, 1908; reissued as *The Up-To-Date Pekingese and All Other Toy Dogs,* Brighton, 1920.

RENNIE, D. F.: *Peking and the Pekingese,* London, 1865, two volumes.

SERGEANT, P. W.: *The Empress Josephine, Napoleon's Enchantress,* London, 1908, two volumes.

SHAW, V. K.: *The Illustrated Book of thc Dog,* London, 1879-81. Valuable for its coloured plates and chapter on early Pugs by Fred Gresham.

SMITH, A. C.: *About Our Dogs,* London, 1931.

SMITH, C. H.: *Dogs,* London, 1839-40.

'STONEHENGE' (see Walsh, J. H.).

TAPLIN, W.: *The Sportsman's Cabinet,* London, 1803-4, two volumes. This important work is illustrated by excellent engravings after Philip Reinagle, R.A.

THRALE (afterwards Piozzi), H. L.: *A Journey through France, Italy and Germany,* London, 1789.

UNTERMEYER, I. and HACKENBROCH, Y.: *The Collection of Irwin Untermeyer,* Volume I—*Meissen and other Continental Porcelain,* London, 1956; Volume *II—Chelsea and other English Porcelain,* London, l957; the text of both by Yvonne Hackenbroch.

VESEY-FITZGERALD, B.: *The Book of the Dog,* London, 1948. This very handsome work contains sections on many well-known and rare breeds yet has no section on the Pug! Mr. Vesey-FitzGerald tells me that he himself had written a Pug section, being a great admirer of the breed, but that owing to last-minute difficulties of publishing, this whole section and some others were accidentally omitted . . . let us hope there will be a further printing of the book and the omissions made good.
The Domestic Dog, London, 1957.

WALSH ('Stonehenge'), J. H.: *The Dog in Health and Disease,* London 1859.
The Dogs of the British Islands, London, 1867.

WATSON, J.: *The Dog Book,* London, 1906, two volumes. Originally published in parts in the U.S.A. this is a very scarce book in Britain and one deserving of being much better known. It contains very many reproductions of old prints and paintings and is invaluable for its historical matter.

WILLIAMS, M. L.: *A Manual of Toy Dogs,* London, 1900.

WILLIAMS, SIR ROGER: *Actions of the Lowe Countries,* London, 1618.

YOUATT, W.: *The Dog,* London, 1845.

Among old journals of particular interest to the Pug enthusiast are the numbers of the *Ladies' Kennel Journal* between 1895 and 1903, because the editor at that time of this lavishly illustrated magazine was Mrs. Stennard-Robinson, first honorary secretary of the Ladies' Kennel Association, and a breeder of black Pugs. Her daughter Myrtle, then a child, was, as 'Miss Mortivals' [even Beilby on p. 413 of his book mentions among leading breeders 'Miss R. Mortivals, Takely, Essex' —Ed.], one of the big names among early exhibitors of blacks. As a result the magazine is full of pictures and information about Pugs, though not surprisingly the blacks get a somewhat unfair coverage as compared with fawns!